STUDIES FOR SMALL GROUPS

LETTERS
FROM
THE LORD OF
HEAVEN

THE SEVEN

CHURCHES

IN ASIA

Revelation 2–3

Edward P. Myers

COLLEGE PRESS
PUBLISHING COMPANY
Joplin, Missouri

Copyright © 1996
College Press Publishing Co.

All Scripture quotations are taken from the
HOLY BIBLE, NEW INTERNATIONAL VERSION®. NIV®.
Copyright © 1973, 1978, 1984 by International Bible Society.
Used by permission of Zondervan Publishing House.
All rights reserved.

International Standard Book Number 0-89900-705-8

CONTENTS

Series introduction 5

Study introduction 7

1. Ephesus: Return to Your First Love 9

2. Smyrna: Be Ready to Suffer 20

3. Pergamum: Champion the Truth 32

4. Thyatira: Follow Righteousness 44

5. Sardis: Be Good on the Inside 54

6. Philadelphia: Take the Open Door 65

7. Laodicea: Be Wholehearted 74

STUDIES FOR SMALL GROUPS

Welcome to the *Studies for Small Groups* series from College Press, which is designed for simplicity of use while giving insight into important issues of the Christian life. Some, like the present volume, will examine a passage of Scripture for the day-to-day lessons we can learn from it. Others are topical studies, using a wide range of Scripture resources.

A number of possible uses could be made of this study. Because there are a limited number of lessons, the format is ideal for new or potential Christians who can begin the study without feeling that they are tied into an overly long commitment. It could also be used for one or two months of weekly studies by a home Bible study group. The series is suitable for individual as well as group study.

Of course, any study is only as good as the effort you put into it. The group leader should study each lesson carefully before the group study session, and if possible, come up with additional Scriptures and other supporting material. Although study questions are provided for each lesson, it would also be helpful if the leader can add his or her own questions.

Neither is it necessary to complete a full lesson in one class period. If the discussion is going well, don't feel that you have to cut it off to fit time constraints, as long as the discussion is related to the topic and not off on side issues.

The present study fills a vital niche in our understanding of the last book of the New Testament. Revelation is normally viewed as a mysterious, perhaps even frightening, book which deals only with the end time. As a result, the book is either ignored or sensationalized. But chapters 2 and 3 need to be viewed in their own light. The 7 churches addressed in the province of Asia had real problems, problems that have recurred in other places throughout the centuries. By studying what they are told, we are better equipped to deal with similar situations when they arise today.

LETTERS FROM HEAVEN

Years ago I fell in love with the "Letters to the Seven Churches of Asia." First introduced to them in a study of the book of Revelation, I was given the assignment (along with others in the class) to produce a sermon outline for each letter. From that initial assignment came a series of sermons I prepared and have presented on several occasions over the years. This material was transcribed from oral presentations and edited to make the written form more readable. As a result I have no way of knowing where I leave off and someone else begins. Each time there was more to learn and additional material used. Over the past twenty years it is difficult for me to remember what belongs to others and what I have, through continued use, made my own. I used several sources, taking careful notes as I prepared to preach and teach on this material. Some I remember, others I do not (I have personally over one hundred commentaries in my library on the book of Revelation). I did not have in mind, at that time, ever putting this into printed form. People who heard this verbally encouraged me to have it made available in a more permanent form. Through years of use one begins to adopt what he has studied and presented so many times that he tends to make it his own. I have not tried to intentionally plagiarize any material. My desire is to make these letters "come alive" for people so they might understand their message. I freely acknowledge that what is presented here is more appropriately a compilation by this writer rather than material written by him. This work is intended to be more devotional than anything else. It is presented for use in classroom and small group discussions. I am trying to be of help in making the material come alive and speak to the heart.

There is really no one who lives without an indebtedness to others. This is certainly true for me. Without the assistance of several individuals this book would never have made it to print. Three different ladies — Robin Tucker, Carol Caveman, and Lou Knox each typed the manuscript at different stages. Their patience in trying to make something readable out of chaos will always be appreciated.

A special thank you goes to Joyce McCartt; her proofreading and marking the manuscript has saved me from many grammatical errors. Susan Cloer of Resource Publications (Searcy, Arkansas) came up with the idea of modernizing the letters and provided the translation used in this presentation. This material was first used in the Truth for Today magazine. Dan Rees suggested subtitles and provided study questions that accompany each chapter. I thank him for his contribution. A colleague, Dr. Don Shackleford, read the page proofs and offered corrections — his eagle eye did not miss much.

To whatever degree this work is improved because of the help of others, I am grateful. However, any remaining deficiencies are mine alone and they are not to be blamed.

I would like to thank Mr. John Hunter and College Press for making this study guide available for a larger audience. John has been more than gracious in his assistance and encouragement in the preparation of this material. I know the schedule he originally planned was earlier than this and the delay was on my part, not his. I hope this material can be used to increase Bible study in general, and of the seven churches of Asia in particular.

Edward P. Myers
Searcy, AR

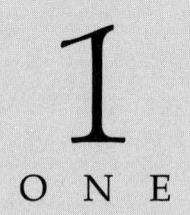

ONE

EPHESUS
RETURN TO YOUR FIRST LOVE

The Church
Ephesus
Asia Minor

Dear Brethren,
    I know your deeds and your toil and perseverance, and that you cannot endure evil men, and you put to the test those who call themselves apostles, and they are not, and you found them to be false; and you have perseverance and have endured for My name's sake, and have not grown weary. But I have this against you, that you have left your first love. Remember therefore from where you have fallen, and repent and do the deeds you did at first; or else I am coming to you, and will remove your lampstand out of its place — unless you repent. Yet this you do have, that you hate the deeds of the Nicolaitans, which I also hate. He who has an ear, let him hear what the Spirit says to the churches. To him who overcomes, I will grant to eat of the tree of life, which is in the Paradise of God.

                                  Lovingly,
                                The One who holds the seven stars
                                in His right hand, the One who walks
                                among the seven golden lampstands

Revelation 2:1-7

THE CITY

Some background information might give us more understanding of the situation at Ephesus.

Commercially: As John writes these words, Ephesus is at the zenith of her greatness. Commercially she is a city of great importance. Located at a very important spot geographically, Ephesus had one of the best harbors of all of Asia Minor. Three main roads, one from the east, one from the west, and another from the south all converged at Ephesus. Those factors combined to make the city a great trading center. One person has called Ephesus "The Vanity Fair of the Ancient World." F.W. Farrar suggests that a picture of Ephesus could be drawn from its markets. In Revelation 18 we see a list of abundant and exotic merchandise, and those would be the kinds of things found in the markets of Ephesus: gold, silver, precious stones, pearls, fine linen and purple silk, scarlet, thyne wood, ivory, brass, iron, marble, cinnamon, spice, incense, ointment, frankincense, wine, oil, fine flour, wheat, cattle, sheep, horses, chariots and slaves. In commerce and in wealth there were few cities that surpassed her. During this period, Ephesus was probably the foremost city in Asia Minor for business and trade.

Politically: Politically, there are three things about Ephesus we need to be aware of.

A Free City. First of all, she was a free city. When Rome conquered a territory, troops were garrisoned in the cities to maintain order. The people of Ephesus decided to transfer their allegiance to Rome and voluntarily pay tribute, so they were granted the status of "free city" which meant they did not have to endure the presence of Roman troops in their city.

An Assize City. Secondly, it was called an assize city. Assize cities were those in which all the important judicial cases were tried. Periodically the Roman Governor would travel to Ephesus for the purpose of hearing important cases, and his visit to the city always stirred up an increase in political activity.

> "He who has an ear, let him hear what the Spirit says to the churches."

The Panionian Games. Thirdly, Ephesus was the site of the Panionian games, which rank with our Olympic games. These public games were open to everyone and were often funded by public officials who were so involved and interested they would bear the cost of the games. Because of this the games soon became political in nature and influence. Commercially and politically Ephesus was a city of great importance.

> **False teachers would never stand in the pulpit of the church at Ephesus and get away with teaching false doctrine.**

Religiously: Ephesus was also a city of religious importance. The Temple of Diana was located in Ephesus, and was one of the seven wonders of the world. The people of Ephesus considered the Temple of Diana their greatest glory. As far back as man's history has been able to record, there has been a temple to Diana in Ephesus. The first is lost in antiquity. The second burned down the night that Alexander the Great was born. The third one was standing in John's time and was a magnificent structure. "The sun sees nothing finer in his course than Diana's Temple."

When the temple was built, the ladies of the city brought their finest jewels to beautify it. Alexander the Great offered all the spoils of his Eastern Campaign for the privilege of having his name inscribed on the temple, but his offer was refused. Only the name of Ephesus could be connected with the Temple of Diana.

Population: Being a seaport its population was mixed, and each nationality had its own section of the city. There were Jews, Greeks, and foreigners as well as the original Athenians.

Biblically: Biblically speaking, we know more about Ephesus and what happened there than we do of the other cities mentioned in Revelation 2 and 3. Paul visited Ephesus on his second missionary journey, and left Aquila and Priscilla there to work with the church (Acts 18:19ff). An eloquent man named Apollos, well versed in Scripture, came to Ephesus and began teaching. Knowing only the baptism of

John, he had to be taught the way of the Lord more perfectly by Aquila and Priscilla.

While Paul was in Ephesus again on his third journey (Acts 19:1ff) opposition grew against him, and that opposition basically took three forms: (1) a hardening of heart among the listeners; (2) imitation; (3) opposition by the worshipers of Diana.

A hardening of heart. The same sun that shines on this earth will either melt ice or harden clay, and the Gospel that is preached of God's Son will either melt the heart and cause one to believe and obey or it will harden the heart. A harding of the heart is one of the forms of opposition Paul met when he was in Ephesus. As Paul preached the Gospel there were some who believed and obeyed, but there were some whose hearts were hardened and who rejected the good news of Jesus.

Imitation. The second form of opposition that was a factor in Paul's ministry in Ephesus was an old trick of the Devil called imitation. Miracles were being done by Paul, and certain Jews rose up to try to mimic those miracles. When seven sons of Sceva tried to cast out a demon in the name of the Lord Jesus, the demon said, "Jesus I know, and Paul I know, but who are you?" (Acts 19:13-16).

Even today the Devil tries through imitation to cause people to be lost. Paul says in 2 Cor. 11:13-15, "For such men are false apostles, deceitful workmen, masquerading as apostles of Christ. And no wonder, for Satan himself masquerades as an angel of light. It is not surprising, then, if his servants masquerade as servants of righteousness. Their end will be what their actions deserve."

Opposition by the worshipers of Diana. The third form of opposition that arose centered around the worship of Diana. The temple itself was a structure of magnificent beauty, but it was the center of idol worship involving immoral sexual activity. In spite of that influence, Paul's preaching was having a great impact on the city (Acts 19:20). A silversmith named Demetrius made silver shrines of Diana, and feared for his livelihood if

> The same sun that shines on this earth will either melt ice or harden clay.

many Ephesians were converted to this new religion. He stirred up a riot that threw the entire city into confusion, and put Paul and his companions at risk. In spite of the opposition, the Gospel was preached, believed and obeyed. While Paul was in Ephesus

> Even today the Devil tries through imitation to cause people to be lost.

those two years the Gospel spread throughout Asia (Acts 19:10), and the church was established and strengthened. There is, perhaps, no more tender passage to be found than Acts 20:17-38 where Luke records Paul's farewell to the elders from Ephesus.

As Paul leaves Ephesus, according to the biblical text, the congregation is a glowing, growing, going church. Thirty years later things have changed, and the message that is revealed to the Apostle John calls for repentance.

It has been said that all it takes is one untaught generation for the church to fall into apostasy. All it takes is one generation who have not been taught the fundamentals of the distinct nature of the New Testament church; the distinct nature of Christian worship; the importance of being in a proper relationship with God in obedience to the Gospel of Jesus Christ. All it takes is one untaught generation and the church is in trouble.

In a short thirty-year time period the church at Ephesus had changed. Acts 18-20 tells us of an active, growing church, but the message to the church in Revelation 2 paints a different picture.

SALUTATION AND SELF-DESIGNATION, 2:1

"To the angel of the church in Ephesus write: These are the words of him who holds the seven stars in his right hand and walks among the seven golden lampstands."

"The angel of the church" — The identity of "the angel of the church" has been interpreted in several ways: (1) heavenly guardians of the church, (2) human representatives of the elders, pastors, or preachers, (3) the personification of the churches themselves, or (4) literally human messengers. It is the judgment of this writer that number three best fits a proper understanding of this phrase.

"Holds the seven stars in his right hand" —We know from Revelation 1 that this is the Lord Jesus Christ. He is the one who holds in his hand the seven stars which are the seven churches. The word translated "hold" is very interesting. There are two different meanings that can be understood from the word "hold." (1) To hold a book in our hand is to hold a corner of the book rather than enclosing the entire book in our hand. (2) To hold a hazel nut or pecan in our hand is to completely enclose or hold the entire object. The second is the construction which is used. The Lord is saying, "I am the one who holds the church totally, all of it, completely in my hand." The destiny of the church belongs to the Lord Jesus Christ. He wants the church to know who is presenting the message, and identifies himself in such a way as to get their attention.

COMMENDATION, 2:2-3, 6

I know your deeds, your hard work and your perseverance. I know that you cannot tolerate wicked men, that you have tested those who claim to be apostles but are not, and have found them false. You have persevered and have endured hardships for my name, and have not grown weary [verses 2 and 3]. . . . But you have this in your favor: You hate the practices of the Nicolaitans, which I also hate [verse 6].

The Lord begins by commending them for what is right in their life. He says two things: (1) you are loyal in your practice; and (2) you are loyal in your doctrine. Three words are significant when we consider their loyalty and practice: "deeds," "hard work," and "perseverance." In practice, they were a working, toiling, patient church. The construction in the original indicates it is not three things that are being said, but one. Jesus is saying, "I know your deeds," that is, your hard work and perseverance. "Hard work and perseverance" identify what the work

> It has been said that all it takes is one untaught generation for the church to fall into apostasy.

is. In practice they are a people loyal to the Lord Jesus Christ as far as their labor is concerned.

They are loyal in doctrine as well. He says, "You tested false apostles and found them to be such, and you hated the work of the Nicolaitans which I also hate." *False teachers would never stand in the pulpit of the church at Ephesus and get away with teaching false doctrine.* The Lord commends them for their faithfulness in this area. We wonder what could be said against a church which has been decribed in this way. Ray Summers makes this observation,

> **We need to be zealous and on fire and doing for the Lord what the first love demands of our life.**

> The entire commendation leaves one inclined to question if there could be anything wrong with such a church. It carried on its services in face of difficulties; it rejected false teachers; it hated sin; it did not grow weary in the Lord's work. That is what one would expect from a church that had been blessed by the services of great leaders: Apollos and Priscilla and Aquila, Timothy, John the Beloved disciple. But the Lord looks with a piercing eye of flame and discovers a great flaw.

For you see, while there is much reason to commend this church, there is also something to condemn. And after the Lord has talked about what is right with the church, then he turns to state what is wrong.

CONDEMNATION, 2:4

"Yet I hold this against you: You have forsaken your first love." What is first love? *First love is what will cause a young man to work all week to make $15 and then go out and spend $20 on his girl.* It is an intense love. First love is the depth of feeling that would cause you to sit up all night with a sick child. It involves zeal, devotion, intensity and commitment. It is that enthusiasm we see when a person becomes a Christian; when they have been redeemed by God's grace in their obedience to the Gospel of Jesus Christ and in response just cannot ever do enough. That is what the Ephesians lost. They lost the enthusiasm that had caused some of them to burn their books on the magical arts when they turned from those practices. Somewhere along the line the zeal, enthusiasm, and love they had at the beginning had diminished — it had grown cold. In other words, the honeymoon was over. The Lord says, "This is what I have against you: you have lost that zeal, that enthusiasm — that first love." They are still loyal in practice: they are working, they are toiling, they are laboring, they are being patient. They are still loyal in doctrine; they would not tolerate a false teacher. But, they were not doing their first works. They had left their first love, and the Lord indicted them for it.

He is going to tell them they need to change. Four words that start with "R" summarize the message the Lord has for them. *He is going to say, Remember, Repent, Repeat, or I am going to Remove.*

WARNING AND JUDGMENT, 2:5-6

Remember. "Remember the height from which you have fallen!" The road back begins by remembering. Remember the story of the prodigal son? He left home, wasted everything he had, and ended up feeding pigs. But he remembered that even the servants in his father's home were in a better situation than he was, so with deep humility he decided to go home and ask to be simply a servant. He did not consider himself worthy of asking to be restored to his place of sonship — he would be content with the position of servant. His restoration began with remembering. The Lord told the Ephesians to remember where they had been.

> First love is what will cause a young man to work all week to make $15 and then go out and spend $20 on his girl.

Repent. Remembering is not enough. We hear people today say, "I remember when we used to have a lot of visiting going on." "I remember when we used to have so many people here you could not put us all in the pews." If we are not careful we could stroll down memory lane toward trouble because we have not repented of our lethargy and gone back to our original zeal. That is exactly what happened at Ephesus. They tightened their belts and girded themselves when it came to false teachers, they manifested works and toil and patience, but the Lord said they had lost their first love. They had lost sight of what should have been number one in their lives: their love for Jesus and doing for him. They were told to remember and repent.

> He is going to say, Remember, Repent, Repeat, or I am going to Remove.

Repeat. Then they were told to repeat. "Remember the height from which you have fallen! Repent [and notice] and do the things you did at first." In other words, repeat in your life what you used to do. Return to that original state of service out of a heart of love. Christ warns that if they do not return to that first state, they are forfeiting their right to exist as a church.

Remove. "If you do not repent, I will come to you and remove your lampstand from its place." The lampstand stood for the existence of the church. The Lord is saying, "You either remember and repent and repeat or I will remove you from having a right to exist as my people and to represent me on earth." That is strong language. It says, in essence, that *we need to be zealous and on fire and doing for the Lord what that first love demands of our life,* or we do not have a right to be his people. "I will remove your lampstand from its place" — that is the judgment which could be brought upon the church.

EXHORTATION AND PROMISE, 2:7b

Exhortation. "He who has an ear, let him hear what the Spirit says to the churches." Even though this was addressed specifically to the church at Ephesus, it was part of a message written to all the churches in Asia Minor. We see this exhortation repeated to each of the seven churches. The message is the same to us as well. Christians today need to be careful to stay out of the category of those "who have eyes, but do not see, and have ears, but do not hear" and instead be those who "hear what the Spirit says to the churches."

Promise. Another statement we see repeated in each letter, with some variation, is a promise to the overcomer. "To him who overcomes, I will give the right to eat from the tree of life, which is in the paradise of God." We were introduced to the tree of life in Gen. 2:9, and Gen. 3:22 gives us some idea of its significance. We run into it again at the close of the book of Revelation in chapter 22.

> Then the angel showed me the river of the water of life, as clear as crystal, flowing from the throne of God and of the Lamb down the middle of the great street of the city. On each side of the river stood the tree of life, bearing twelve crops of fruit, yielding its fruit every month. And the leaves of the tree are for the healing of the nations [verses 1 and 2]. . . . Blessed are those who wash their robes, that they may have the right to come to the tree of life and may go through the gates into the city [verse 14]. . . . And if anyone takes words away from this book of prophecy, God will take away from him his share in the tree of life and in the holy city, which are described in this book [verse 19].

Adam and Eve could have eaten of the tree of life and lived forever in the Garden of Eden if they had heeded what they were told. The message to the Ephesians is that their reward will be eating of the tree of life in the Paradise of God if they act on what they have been told.

The overcoming passage applies to Christians today as well as to those to whom it was written. We overcome by heeding the words of the Lord, just as the Ephesians were told to do. They were told to remember and repent and repeat, so the Lord would not remove. The Lord began and ended the letter on a positive note. He praised them first, then chastised them for their shortcomings, and finally ended with a message of hope. The indictment against them was serious. They had left their first love; they were not serving the Lord with the love, zeal and enthusiasm they had at first. But if they will overcome and go back to their first works, then he will

> Adam and Eve could have eaten of the tree of life and lived forever in the Garden of Eden if they had heeded what they were told.

give them the right to eat of the tree of life, which is in the paradise of God.

REFLECTING ON EPHESUS

1. What does it mean to say that "All it takes is one generation and the church is in trouble"? What can be done to prevent such a disaster?

2. What made Ephesus such an important city? Can you think of parallels today?

3. Is it inevitable for love to gradually decrease? What can keep love alive?

4. What was your "first love" for God like? How is your present state different?

5. Who might be the "Nicolaitans" of today? Do we hate their practices?

6. Discuss what it would be like if Adam and Eve had not been expelled from the Garden of Eden.

7. What eventually happened to the church in Ephesus? Does it seem as though they heeded the warning of this letter?

8. If you had to summarize this letter, how would you do so, in your own words?

2
TWO

SMYRNA
BE READY TO SUFFER

The Church
Smyrna
Asia Minor

Dear Brethren,
   I know your tribulation and your poverty (but you are rich), and the blasphemy by those who say they are Jews and are not, but are a synagogue of Satan. Do not fear what you are about to suffer. Behold, the devil is about to cast some of you into prison, that you may be tested, and you will have tribulation ten days. Be faithful until death, and I will give you the crown of life. He who has an ear, let him hear what the Spirit says to the churches. He who overcomes shall not be hurt by the second death.

                        Lovingly,
                        The first and the last, who was dead,
                        and has come to life

Revelation 2:8-11

The letter to the church at Smyrna is unique. Not only is it the shortest of the seven letters; it is one of only two letters which has no words of condemnation. *These four short verses are power-packed, containing information and words of encouragement badly needed by the brethren who were the faithful in Christ at Smyrna.*

THE CITY

We can better appreciate what is said here if we know something about the city of Smyrna. If we lived in Asia Minor at that time and in the city of Smyrna, what would have been our impressions of the city?

> These verses contain information and words of encouragement badly needed by the brethren who were faithful in Christ at Smyrna.

A Great Trade City. If you had lived in Asia Minor in those days you would have been aware of the fact that Smyrna was a great trade city. She stood on a deep gulf thirty-five miles north of Ephesus, and had a magnificent harbor which was especially valuable during times of war because it could be enclosed. The city stood at the end of a road which served the valley of the river Hermus, and all the trade of the valley passed through its harbor. The climate was conducive to the growing of grapes, among other crops, and trade in wine contributed to her wealth.

A Beautiful City. Smyrna was an outstandingly beautiful city. She was famous for the wide paved streets which ran from one end of the city to the other. The most well-known of her thoroughfares was called "Golden Street," and along this lovely avenue stood many imposing heathen temples; she was a city filled with religious idolatry. On Golden Street toward the sea end of the city was the great Temple of Cybele. As the road headed through the city toward the foothills many other temples lined its way, including temples to the god Asklepios and the goddess Aphrodite. In the inland foothills was the Temple of Zeus. These temples were magnificent structures and added to Smyrna's reputation for beauty and glory.

Smyrna possessed a famous stadium, an impressive library, and claimed to have the largest public theater in all of Asia Minor. She claimed to be the birthplace of the ancient Greek poet Homer, and a monument to him stood in the city. No wonder this splendid city was known as "the glory of Asia."

An Important Political City. Smyrna was on the winning side in all the civil wars that took place during her history, and

Rome was not unmindful of that. She was granted the status of free city — allowing her to govern herself and be free of garrisons of Roman troops, and assize city — giving her the stature of being an important judicial and political center. People were allowed to go about their day-to-day activities as normal as long as allegiance was given to Rome.

DIFFICULTIES FOR CHRISTIANS

It may sound like Smyrna was an ideal place to live, but there were two factors that made life there very difficult for Christians.

Emperor Worship. The first was emperor worship. As Rome conquered more and more of the world, she allowed vassal peoples to govern themselves as long as they were loyal to Rome and faithfully paid their taxes. She did, however, strive to unify conquered peoples, and their aim was to accomplish this unity through a national religion. It could not be done with any of the existing religions because of the diversity of gods and practices.

This led to the concept of *Dea Roma* — the goddess of Rome. The worship of Rome itself as a deity was conceived as a unifying force. Issuing from this was the worship of Caesar. Since the Caesar represented the nation of Rome to the people, the Caesars began to look upon themselves as gods. Early in Rome's history the Caesars were not deified until after their death, but Caligula, who became emperor in A.D. 37, changed that precedent by declaring himself divine during his reign. In the years following, emperor worship became firmly established and Domitian (A.D. 81-96), declared himself to be god in the flesh.

Christians were put in a difficult position because refusal to participate in emperor worship resulted in persecution.

Once a year every citizen of the Roman empire (including Smyrna) was required to place a pinch of incense on the altar to the emperor, say the words "Caesar is lord," and receive a token as evidence that the worship had been performed. It was a very brief ceremony, taking perhaps thirty seconds.

Christians were put in a difficult position because refusal to participate in emperor worship resulted in persecution. Some began to practice a device called "mental reservation." They rationalized that as long as they acknowledged in their minds that Jesus was Lord, it would be all right to comply with the requirements of emperor worship and be protected against the persecution or even death which might result from their refusal. They felt it would not be wrong to say "Caesar is lord" under those circumstances, even though they did not agree with the statement. Rome would not object to that — as long as a person went through the motions to demonstrate their loyalty to Rome, it did not matter to the authorities what god he worshipped. Caesar worship was not so much a question of religious loyalty as it was political loyalty.

> **The conscientious Christian risked political and economic persecution and possible arrest for treason.**

The conscientious Christian who refused to participate in any way risked political and economic persecution and possible arrest for treason.

A Large Jewish Population. The large Jewish population was the second factor which created difficulties for the Christians in Smyrna. The Jews informed on Christians to the local governor, and used their influence to persuade him to unleash an attack on Christianity. This issued in severe persecutions, even to the point of martyrdom for some. The most famous historical personage who died a martyr's death in Smyrna was Polycarp, Bishop of Smyrna. It was a multitude of people that cried for Polycarp to be found, arrested and condemned to death. The Jews cried along with the Gentiles this accusation against Polycarp, "This is the teacher of Asia, the father of Christians, the destroyers of our gods, the one who teaches many not to sacrifice nor to worship" (*The Martyrdom of Polycarp* 12.2, in *The Apostolic Fathers*, Thomas Nelson Publishers, 1978). As he entered the arena he was instructed to recant his faith in Christ. He acknowledged that he was a Christian and gave this response, *"I have served him eighty-six years and in no way has he dealt unjustly with me; so how can I blaspheme my king who saved me?"* (*Martyrdom* 9.3).

The Jews not only demanded his arrest, but even though it was the Sabbath they led the mob in gathering the sticks to burn Polycarp to death. "You threaten fire which burns for a hour," Polycarp said, "and is soon quenched; for you are ignorant of the fire of the coming judgment and eternal punishment reserved for the wicked. But why do you wait? Come, do what you will!" (*Martyrdom* 11.2). As he was being burned he prayed, "I bless you because you have considered me worthy of this day and hour to receive a portion, among the number of the martyrs, in the cup of your Christ unto the resurrection of eternal life . . ." (*Martyrdom* 14.2).

And so Polycarp died, and it was the Jews primarily who were responsible for his death.

Keeping this background material in mind will help us better understand the significance of some of the things said in the letter.

SALUTATION AND SELF-DESIGNATION, 2:8

"To the angel of the church in Smyrna write: These are the words of him who is the First and the Last, who died and came to life again." As he does in the other letters, the Lord identifies himself as the writer of this letter by using a description applied to him earlier. In Rev. 1:17-18 John says, "When I saw him, I fell at his feet as though dead. Then he placed his right hand on me and said: 'Do not be afraid. *I am the First and the Last. I am the Living One; I was dead, and behold, I am alive for ever and ever!* And I hold the keys of death and Hades.'"

Christians in Smyrna faced severe persecutions because of emperor worship and because of the hatred of the Jews.

> "In no way has he dealt unjustly with me; so how can I blaspheme my king who saved me?"

What a great ray of hope it must been to read, "To the angel of the church in Smyrna write: These are the words of him who is the First and the Last, who was dead and who lives again." That is what the original language literally says — "who was dead and who lives again." The writer was one who had victory over death, and that was especially meaningful to people who knew they faced the possibility of death.

> "I am the First and the Last. I am the Living One; I was dead, and behold, I am alive for ever and ever!"

The Lord identifies himself as "the first and the last, who was dead and lives again." Thus he tells them that he has been through what they are suffering. He is well qualified to comfort them and bring them assurance from firsthand knowledge.

COMMENDATION, 2:9-10a

Listen to the beautiful words of commendation. "I know your afflictions and your poverty — yet you are rich! I know the slander of those who say they are Jews, and are not, but are a synagogue of Satan."

Afflictions. The word "affliction" in the original means pressure that is brought to bear upon someone from without. It carries the idea of grapes in a winepress that were crushed by pressure or by trampling of feet. It was used of a man being crushed to death by the weight of a great boulder. G.K. Chesterton has said it was the sign of a real man that he could pass the breaking point and not break.

The Lord is telling the Christians at Smyrna he knows what they are going through, and he understands. The message he has for them will help them cope with the pressures of tribulation.

Poverty. Then he says, "I know your poverty." There are two words in the original language for one who is poor. *Penia* means a person who could afford nothing beyond the barest necessities of life. He and his family might have the minimum of food, clothing and shelter, but nothing in addition to that.

Ptocheia is the word used here and specifically identifies one who could not even afford the necessities of life. Why were the Christians in Smyrna that poor? Remember emperor worship? Doing business in Smyrna depended on having that little token which proved a person was loyal to Caesar. People without the token were blacklisted. Merchants were afraid they would be in danger if they dealt with customers who were considered disloyal to the state. The result was deep poverty for the Christians at Smyrna.

Notice the parenthesis there: "I know your afflictions, and your poverty — yet you are rich!" *According to the world's standards they are in terrible shape, undergoing persecution and suffering poverty, but by the Lord's standards they are rich.*

The word for "rich" here is the word from which we get the English words "plutarchy," "plutocrat," "plutocracy," etc., conveying the idea of being in a position of power and authority because of wealth. The Lord is telling them that in spite of their situation in the world's eyes, in the eyes of heaven's Banker they are rich in a spiritual way, and have power because of that wealth.

That thought is in line with what other passages in the New Testament tell us. In Luke 12:15 Jesus said, ". . . a man's life does not consist in the abundance of his possessions." In Matt. 6:19-21 he said, "Do not store up for yourselves treasures on earth, where moth and rust destroy, and where thieves break in and steal. But store up for yourselves treasures in heaven, where moth and rust do not destroy, and where thieves do not break in and steal. For where your treasure is, there your heart will be also."

They were, by their life and their faithfulness to the Lord Jesus Christ, showing they were rich as far as heaven's bank account was concerned.

Slander. Then Jesus refers to those who slander the Christians in Smyrna — those who claim to be Jews but are not, but are a synagogue of Satan. The word used for "slander" is the Greek word *blasphemia*, from which we get our word "blasphemy," and it means "to speak against." As we saw in the background study, the Jews in Smyrna informed on the Christians to the Roman officials, and used their influence with those

> According to the world's standards, they are in terrible shape, but by the Lord's standards they are rich.

officials to cause the Christians to be persecuted.

The Jews may have had a sign over their place of worship which said "Synagogue of the Lord," but Jesus said they were a "synagogue of Satan." They may have claimed to be God's people, but in reality they belonged to the devil. A lot of people claim to be Christians today, but if that is not the Lord's evaluation of them, they belong to Satan.

> They would have to bear as much persecution as a human could withstand, but only for a short time.

The Lord's words must have comforted the Christians at Smyrna. He knew the true nature of the Jews, and justice would be done. The Jews would be punished for their blasphemy, and the Christians would be rewarded for their faithfulness.

Persecution. The Christians at Smyrna have endured tribulation, poverty, and slander — and there is more to come. "Do not be afraid of what you are about to suffer. I tell you, the devil will put some of you in prison to test you, and you will suffer persecution for ten days" (verse 10). Here are people going through tribulation, or pressure beyond what some are able to bear; here are people poverty stricken because they are loyal to Jesus Christ; here are people being slandered. Jesus did not tell them things would get better, but that they would get worse. Some of them are going to be cast into prison by the devil and tried, and they would have tribulation ten days.

The phrase "ten days" indicates a period of short duration. It is, however, complete in its persecution. Numbers are significant in the book of Revelation. The number five represented human completeness. A man looked at his hands and saw that five fingers each made his hands complete. Ten is human completeness doubled. *They would have to bear as much persecution as a human could withstand, but only for a short time.*

Martyrdom. With the tribulation, poverty, slander and persecution also came martyrdom. We have already seen what happened to Polycarp. Verse 10 continues, "Be faithful, even to the point of death, and I will give you the crown of life."

Some take this verse to mean, "Be faithful until the day you die, and I will give you the crown of life." That is a true statement, but not what this verse says. In the construction of the original language here, the word "unto," translated "even to the point of" in the NIV, causes the sentence to mean, "Be faithful knowing that your faithfulness will cause your death." The message to the Christians at Smyrna was much stronger than being told they would be rewarded for remaining faithful to the end of their lives. They were being told they would be rewarded for a faithfulness which would actually be the cause of their death. This may sound like a frightening message, but consider the one who is addressing them. Look at verse 8, "These are the words of him who is the First and the Last, who died and came to life again." The message is coming from the One who himself had overcome death, and he is telling them not to be afraid. With those words of encouragement their faith could cause them to remain steadfast even if it meant their death.

It is hard for Christians today to relate to the possibility of dying for our faith in Christ. Perhaps if we try to picture ourselves being threatened with death unless we deny Christ, or one of our children being threatened with death unless we deny Christ, we can better understand what the Christians in Smyrna were going through and what this message meant to them.

EXHORTATION AND PROMISE, 2:10b, 11

Exhortation. "He who has an ear, let him hear him hear what the Spirit says to the churches." This phrase is found at the close of each of the letters (cf. 2:7, 11, 17, 29; 3:6, 13, 22). The primary instruction found in each letter is for the specific need of that particular church. *However, the lessons to be learned are not limited to that particular church but should be for all the churches.* That is to say, what is said to the church at Ephesus is just as applicable to Smyrna, Laodicea, Thyatira, etc. and vice versa. The lessons God wants learned at one church are just as important for other churches facing similar situations.

> **Being faithful unto death and overcoming are the same thing.**

Promise. In spite of the serious subject of the letter, it is actually one of hope and consolation. They were promised the "crown of life" if they were faithful unto death.

There are two words for "crown" in the Greek. *Diademos* signified a ruling crown, that worn by royalty. *Stephanos* had three applications: (1) the victory crown, given to the winner of a competition; (2) the festal crown, worn at weddings and other festive occasions; and (3) the laurel crown given for faithful civic service.

The idea of a "crown of life" may embody all three of these applications, but in particular we think of the victory crown. The faithful in Smyrna are being told they will be victorious. Their faithfulness may bring about death, but it will be rewarded with victory.

More words of hope and comfort are found in the last part of verse 11. Jesus says, "He who overcomes will not be hurt at all by the second death." We are given more information about the "second death" in Revelation 20. Verse 6 reads, "Blessed and holy are those who have part in the first resurrection. The second death has no power over them . . ." What is that second death? We find it explained in verse 14, "Then death and Hades were thrown into the lake of fire. The lake of fire is the second death."

The Christians of Smyrna were told not to fear the death of the body, because those who overcame would not face the second death. Everyone's physical body is going to die unless Jesus returns first, but we do not need to be afraid of that death. The second death is the one we need to fear, but the Lord promises victory over that death to those who overcome.

Being faithful unto death and overcoming are the same thing. In each one of the letters to the seven churches we see the reward to the overcomer stated in a different way. The Christians in Ephesus were promised the right to eat of the tree of life. The Christians in Smyrna are told they will not be hurt by the second death. Each different and beautiful promise means the same thing: eternal victory. And so the letter ends.

It is not likely that Christians today will face the kind of persecution those at Smyrna faced, but no life is completely free of tribulation. The message for today is the same as the one for the first century. Stand firm and face what has to be faced knowing the Lord understands and will bring about justice; be steadfast in the faith; and be confident of the ultimate reward which is more than worth whatever has to be endured.

REFLECTING ON SMYRNA

1. What is different about this letter from the other six?

2. What difficulties did Christians face in Smyrna?

3. Do we have modern equivalents to the emperor worship of John's day?

4. How can we emulate Polycarp if we do not face literal martyrdom by fire?

5. What is the significance of the description of Jesus in this letter?

6. What is the promise to the overcomers of Smyrna? Do you expect to receive a crown?

7. What is your reaction when those who should be God's most able helpers seem instead to be causing the greatest problems?

8. Please produce your own summary of this letter.

THREE

PERGAMUM
CHAMPION THE TRUTH

The Church
Pergamum
Asia Minor

Dear Brethren,
I know where you dwell, where Satan's throne is; and you hold fast My name, and did not deny My faith, even in the days of Antipas. My witness, My faithful one, who was killed among you, where Satan dwells. But I have a few things against you, because you have there some who hold the teaching of Balaam, who kept teaching Balak to put a stumbling block before the sons of Israel, to eat things sacrificed to idols, and to commit acts of immorality. Thus you also have some who in the same way hold the teaching of the Nicolaitans. Repent therefore; or else I am coming to you quickly, and I will make war against them with the sword of My mouth. He who has an ear, let him hear what the Spirit says to the churches. To him who overcomes, to him I will give some of the hidden manna, and I will give him a white stone, and a new name written on the stone which no one knows but he who receives it.

Lovingly,
The One who has the sharp
two-edged sword

Revelation 2:12-17

THE CITY

In this letter he identifies himself as "him who has the sharp double-edged sword."

History. Travel north from the city of Smyrna forty miles, then go inland fifteen miles to the Caicus valley, and you will find the city of Pergamum. This city of Mysia had been a capital city since the time of the Attalid Empire (circa 231 B.C.) which was broken during the days of the rule and conquest of Alexander the Great. In 133 B.C., her dying king bequeathed her to the possession of the Roman Empire, and she became the chief city of the new province of Asia.

Pergamum never attained to the commercial eminence or the trade position of either Ephesus or Smyrna, but she was far superior in historical greatness. In fact, historically she was considered to be the greatest city of Asia Minor. Her prestige caused her to be the site of the first temple of the Caesar-cult, erected to Rome and Augustus in 29 B.C., and a second temple was later erected to Trajan. Pliny, the Roman writer, called it *longe clarissimum Asiae*, the most famous city of Asia. Pergamum had the atmosphere of an ancient capital city with the pride of centuries of greatness behind it.

Important Library. One of Pergamum's claims to fame was her magnificent library. Two hundred thousand volumes were housed in this famous institution. That many volumes would constitute a large library by anyone's estimation, but it is even more impressive when we consider that in those days books were all handwritten. Two hundred thousand handwritten volumes is an extraordinary collection. It is noteworthy that Pergamum's library rivaled that of Alexandria, and there was some competition between the two cities as to which library was the greatest. Parchment was invented at Pergamum because Egypt banned the export of papyrus. Because of the library, Pergamum was a focal point of intellectual and scholastic activities.

Paganism. Pergamum was also well-known as a center of worship to the gods Asklepios, Zeus, Dionysus and Athena. The symbol of Asklepios was a serpent, and coins of the city with serpents on them demonstrated the interconnection between religion and politics. A healing cult revolved around Asklepios, and invalids from all over Asia traveled to Pergamum to be healed in his temple. There was a school of medicine connected with the temple. A throne-like altar to Zeus stood on a crag above the city, and the friezes are now in the Berlin Museum. As if Christians in Pergamum would not have been offended enough by the worship of an image of a snake, Asklepios was called "the Savior." *The alliance between politics and paganism would have put a lot of pressure on Christians to compromise*, and created a favorable climate for Nicolaitanism.

Knowing those things about Pergamum gives us some insight into the message the Lord had for the Christians who lived there.

SALUTATION AND SELF-DESIGNATION, 2:12

In verse 12 we see the salutation and self-designation with which the Lord begins each of these letters. *In this letter he identifies himself as "him who has the sharp double-edged sword."* That description from Rev. 1:16 is another among the several picturesque and majestic ways the risen and exalted Christ is depicted in that chapter.

COMMENDATION, 2:13

> I know where you live — where Satan has his throne. Yet you remain true to my name. You did not renounce your faith in me, even in the days of Antipas, my faithful witness, who was put to death in your city — where Satan lives.

The Lord has a threefold commendation for this church. (1) "I know where you dwell." In other words, I am aware of the circumstances under which you have to live. (2) "You remain true to my name" — in spite of the pressures they had not forsaken Christ. (3) "You did not renounce your faith in me" — they

> **The alliance between politics and paganism would have put a lot of pressure on Christians to compromise.**

had not succumbed to emperor or pagan worship. The word "renounce" is in the aorist tense in the original language and has reference to one particular action completed in past time. Evidently there had been a specific period of persecution and crisis during which the Christians of Pergamum had remained true. They did not deny the faith even though the situation was so critical it resulted in the death of one called Antipas, whom the Lord calls his faithful witness. There is no more information about the death of Antipas except a legend which says he was roasted to death inside a brazen bull.

> Antipas may have suffered a martyr's death, but he gained the martyr's reward.

The Lord told the Christians at Smyrna to be faithful even if it cost them their lives, and their reward would be the crown of life (Rev. 2:10). It seems the Christians here in Pergamum faced a similar situation. In speaking here of the death of Antipas the Lord calls him his faithful witness. *Antipas may have suffered a martyr's death, but he gained the martyr's reward.* In Rev. 1:5 John refers to Jesus as "the faithful witness." It is noteworthy that Antipas was described with a title which had been applied to the Lord himself.

Satan's Throne. The Christians at Pergamum dwelled "where Satan's throne is." The Greek word *thronos* is used in different ways in Scripture and never has reference simply to a place to sit. In Matt. 19:28 it refers to the seat of a judge. In Luke 1:32 it is used in the sense of the throne of a king. It implies a position of power and authority. *Satan did not just exist in Pergamum; he had power and authority there.* There are several possibilities as to what this throne might have reference to in light of the historical background we have already seen.

There are some who believe that this has reference to the great throne — such as the altar of Zeus that overlooked the city from the citadel. Others believe the primary reference is to the cult of Asklepios, the god of healing. He was called Asklepios *Soter*, the Savior god, and his symbol was a serpent. This symbol, of course, obviously would remind

Christians of Satan. We find that imagery in Rev. 12:9 and 20:2. The city was on a hill which looked like a giant throne if approached from the south. From this there are those who believe the city itself would be the throne of this pagan god.

Probably the best understanding of "Satan's throne" is that Pergamum was the center of emperor worship in Asia. As Rome had become the center of Satan's activities in the West, so Pergamum had become the very throne of Satan in the East.

Like Smyrna, Pergamum was the headquarters of one of those presbyteries in which the Caesar worship had been organized. One of the oddest titles a city could be given was *neokoros*, or "temple sweeper." When a city erected a temple to a god, its greatest claim to honor was that it officially became the *neokoros*, the temple sweeper of that god. Of course, the sweeping of the temple was the most menial and humble of religious duties. Behind the title lies the lovely concept that it was a city's greatest privilege to render the humblest service to the god who had taken up his residence within it. Pergamum was a city which called itself the neokoros of the temple where Caesar was worshipped. She was a city where Caesar worship was at its most intense, a city dedicated to glorying in the worship of Caesar. *That, to a Christian, would be nothing less than the worship of Satan.*

In Pergamum it was supremely perilous to be a Christian. Some lived in cities where they were relatively safe most of the year and were only in real danger during the time appointed for the ceremony of worship to Caesar. In Pergamum a Christian's life was in jeopardy every day. He put his life on the line for sake of loyalty to Jesus Christ. In other words, on a day-to-day basis, they were living where Satan was in control.

Live. The Greek word that is translated "live" and "lives" in verse 13 is *katoikein* and conveys the idea of a permanent residence. The Christians there were not just visiting or temporarily sojourning, that was their fixed place of abode. And it was Satan's fixed place of abode as well. The Christians could not leave

> **Satan did not just exist in Pergamum; he had power and authority there.**

and find a place where they could live in peace — they had to endure where they were. They were living in Hell's Headquarters and the Lord commended them for their faithfulness in the face of such adversity.

> To a Christian, worship of Caesar would be nothing less than the worship of Satan.

CONDEMNATION, 2:14-15

In spite of their loyalty and faithfulness in the face of extreme pressure and danger, the Christians at Pergamum needed correction. The Lord said, "I have a few things against you."

The Teaching of Balaam.

> You have people there who hold to the teaching of Balaam, who taught Balak to entice the Israelites to sin by eating food sacrificed to idols and by commiting sexual immorality.

Balaam is an interesting character. His story is told in Numbers 22-25, and he is mentioned in many other places in both the Old and New Testaments. Balaam was a prophet of God with the gift of eloquent speech. He wanted to be true to God, but he also wanted to take advantage of an offer of material wealth and position. As the Israelites traveled from Egypt to the Promised Land, their numbers and victories struck fear into the hearts of the nations they approached, including Moab and Midian. Balak, king of Moab, conspired with the leaders of Midian to hire Balaam the prophet to curse the Israelites so they might be driven out of the land. Jehovah put the words in Balaam's mouth, and instead of curses, Balaam spoke blessings.

Having failed in his attempts to curse the people of God, he gave Balak advice that would result in their corruption. We know from Num. 31:16 and Rev. 2:14 that Balaam was responsible for counseling Balak to lead the Israelites into the immorality and idolatry that is recorded in Numbers 25. As a result of that sin, twenty-four thousand Israelites died. Balaam was killed later when Jehovah ordered Moses to take vengeance on the Midianites.

What is the teaching of Balaam? Balaam probably told the Israelites they could do whatever they wanted without fear of reprisal because they were God's chosen people. He became the prototype of false teachers who would lead Christians into compromise with worldly ideologies. *Balaamism would say that Christian liberty allowed participation in worldly activities* — being saved by grace meant freedom from the moral law. The word for that doctrine today is antinomianism. A little poem goes,

> Freedom from sin, oh happy condition,
> I can sin as I please and still have remission.

Eating meat sacrificed to idols often involved social occasions. It was not uncommon for the participant to take his offering to the temple, offer a few hairs from the forehead of the animal to the idol, then prepare the rest of the animal for a meal for his family, friends, and neighbors. Invitations might even be issued: "Friend, I invite you to dine with me at the temple of our Lord Serapis." Could a Christian share in a social occasion that was held in the temple of the heathen god? Could a Christian partake of the table of demons as well as the table of the Lord? Paul said no, 1 Cor. 10:18-22. The false teachers said yes and encouraged the Christians to compromise.

What we would call fornication and sin were accepted practices in the ancient world. Demosthenes said,

> We have courtesans for the sake of pleasure; we have concubines for the sake of daily cohabitation; we have wives for the purpose of having children legitimately, and for having a faithful guardian over our household affairs.

Sexual promiscuity was not shocking; being told it was wrong was shocking. Immorality was the norm, and those who abstained were set apart and looked upon with suspicion.

> **Balaamism would say that Christian liberty allowed participation in worldly activities.**

There are worldly Christians today who would try to justify participating in sinful activities by citing their liberty in Christ. They wrest the Scriptures to their advantage by quoting the half of a verse that says, "All things are lawful," and omitting the half that says, "but all things are not expedient." The Lord will hold this against Christians today just as he did when he wrote the church at Pergamum.

> There are worldly Christians today who would try to justify participation in sinful activities by citing their liberty in Christ.

The Teaching of the Nicolaitans. Not much is known about the sect of the Nicolaitans from Scripture, but they are mentioned frequently in post-apostolic literature. Apparently their practices and teachings were similar to those of the Balaamites. They seemed to advocate participation in the pagan practices and cooperation with Rome. A Christian who would join in the pagan feasts by eating the meat which had been offered to the idol and indulging in the immoral activities would be safe from the dangers he might incur by setting himself apart and identifying himself as a Christian. A Christian who went along with the rites of emperor worship would be safe from the wrath of Rome. It is easy to see why this teaching might be attractive to some of the Christians in Pergamum.

WARNING AND JUDGMENT, 2:16

Repent. The Christians in Pergamum are given a strong warning, "Repent therefore! Otherwise I will soon come to you." What are they to repent of? They were tolerating sin; there were those who were advocating compromise with pagan practices and emperor worship, and the church was looking the other way. The church at Corinth had a similar problem when it tolerated a man's taking his father's wife, 1 Corinthians 5. The Lord says in essence, "If you don't deal with these Balaamites, I will."

Toleration of sin is a problem in the church today just as it was then. Tolerating what God condemns and looking the other way without taking action is just as much of a sin today as it was then. Christians are to abhor that which is evil, abstain from the very appearance of evil, and not sit by and watch it grow. The church needs to be guarded against the infection of worldliness. Paul said, "A little yeast works through the whole batch of dough," 1 Cor. 5:6.

The Bible teaches that discipline is to be exercised when there is sin in the church (Rom. 16:17; 1 Cor. 5:13; 2 Thess. 3:14; Titus 3:10). It is painful and difficult for all involved but necessary for the purity of the church, and for the restoration of the individuals involved in sin. Pergamum was in the midst of intense and severe persecution, and some of the Christians took the safe road and compromised with the evil. Even today people sometimes discourage preaching against sin lest that preaching cause offense or stir up trouble.

"The sword of my mouth." The Lord tells the Christians at Pergamum that if they do not deal with the Balaamites and Nicolaitans, he will "fight against them with the sword of my mouth." This is the second time the phrase "the sword of my mouth" occurs in this letter (cf. v. 12). Living in a provincial capital where the proconsul was granted the "right of the sword" *the Lord reminds the church that ultimate power over life and death belongs to him.* He will deal with the evil if they will not. In Numbers 22 the Angel of Jehovah met Balaam with a drawn sword (v. 31). Num. 31:8 gives the account of Balaam's death by the sword of the men of Israel. The judgment mentioned here is a judgment in time; a judgment that was imminent to the church in Pergamum, especially in light of the fact that judgment was about to be unleashed upon the whole world (cf. Rev. 3:10).

The spirit of Balaam gets into the church in many ways. Balaam tried to stand with God and at the same time collect a reward from the ungodly. *Today some Christians try to stand with God while at the same time they enjoy the pleasures of the world.* Paul teaches forcefully in 2 Cor. 6:14-7:1 that the church is to be separate from the world. There can be no fellowship between righteousness and iniquity or light and darkness; there is no harmony between Christ and Belial; believers have nothing in common with unbelievers; there can be no agreement between Christians who are the temple of God, and idols. We cannot sing, "There is no other way but the way of the Cross" if we are unwilling to "bid farewell to the ways of the world." We cannot take our stand "beneath the Cross of Jesus" unless we are "content to let the world go by." We cannot properly "survey the wondrous Cross" and not "sacrifice the vain things that charm us most to his blood." We cannot sing from the heart, "Whiter than snow," if we are unwilling for the Lord to "break down every idol and cast out every foe."

> The Bible teaches that discipline is to be exercised when there is sin in the church.

EXHORTATION AND PROMISE, 2:17B

As in all the letters, the Lord says, "He who has an ear, let him hear what the Spirit says to the churches." The message is for all to take to heart. The letter closes with a twofold exhortation and promise.

The Hidden Manna. "To him who overcomes, I will give some of the hidden manna." Manna was the food provided by God for the Israelites as they traveled from Egypt to the Promised Land. There was a Jewish tradition which said the pot of manna in the ark was taken by Jeremiah at the time of the destruction of the temple and hidden underground to be returned to the ark and a new messianic temple. Another tradition held that there is a treasury of manna in heaven which will come down to feed the blessed during the messianic kingdom. In John 6:31ff Jesus draws a parallel between the manna with which God fed the Israelites and himself as the bread of life come down from heaven. The Christians of John's day might have understood "hidden manna" to be spiritual nourishment provided by the Lord himself at a time of victory, as contrasted with the food from sacrifices to idols which the Balaamites were encouraging them to eat.

The White Stone. The one who overcame was not only going to be given the hidden manna, but he was also to be given "a white stone with a new name written on it, known only to him who receives it."

The idea of the white stone was significant in several different ways in the ancient world. A white stone symbolized innocence and might be given to one who had been acquitted of a charge. He could carry that as proof of his acquittal. A white stone was also given to a slave who was granted freedom, and was a sign to all that he was a free man. The victor of a race or contest was given a white stone. A white stone was given to a soldier or warrior who came back from a victorious battle. Among other customs involving a white stone was its use as admission to a banquet. It may be that all of these concepts are inherent in the Lord giving a white stone to the overcomer. It would symbolize their innocence, freedom in Christ, final victory, and admission to the marriage supper of the Lamb.

There are several views on the identity of the "new name." Some think it is the name of Christ. Others think it is the victorious Christian himself. The Lord said no one would know the name except the one who received it. Whatever the new name is, the Christian will know it when he receives the ultimate reward for overcoming.

The message to the Christians at Pergamum applies to Christians today as well. We can feel very complacent and spiritual when we meet together on Sunday for worship, but after Sunday comes Monday. We are back on the job or back at school — out in the world with influences that constantly bombard us and ask us to compromise our principles in living for Jesus Christ. The Lord knows "where we live." He knows we live in a world under the influence of Satan, but he expects us to overcome — to remain faithful and not compromise. The Bible teaches that we are to be a people separated from the ways of this world. It calls upon Christians to live a better life, to walk on a higher plain. The doctrine of Balaamism would have Christians hold hands with God on one side and the devil on the other, and it will result in the wrath of God today just as it did in Pergamum.

> The Lord reminds the church that ultimate power over life and death belongs to him.

REFLECTING ON PERGAMUM

1. How is Jesus described in this letter? Note how this fits in with the overall description in Rev. 1:12-18.

2. What were Pergamum's chief claims to fame? Were they an advantage or a disadvantage as far as God was concerned?

3. What were the two threats to the church's health presented here?

4. Did the earlier martyrdom of Antipas benefit the existing Pergamum church in any way?

5. Is Balaamism a problem today? How would you define Balaamism?

6. Discuss how yeast or leaven can be a symbol both of the church (Matt. 13:33) and of false doctrine (Matt. 16:6; 1 Cor. 5:6).

7. Explain the three gifts promised to the overcomer.

8. Summarize God's message to the church in Pergamum.

4
FOUR

THYATIRA
FOLLOW RIGHTEOUSNESS

The Church
Thyatira
Asia Minor

Dear Brethren,
   I know your deeds, and your love and faith and service and perseverance, and that your deeds of late are greater than at first. But I have this against you, that you tolerate the woman Jezebel, who calls herself a prophetess, and she teaches and leads My bond-servants astray, so that they commit acts of immorality and eat things sacrificed to idols. And I gave her time to repent; and she does not want to repent of her immorality. Behold, I will cast her upon a bed of sickness, and those who commit adultery with her into great tribulation, unless they repent of her deeds. And I will kill her children with pestilence; and all the churches will know that I am He who searches the minds and hearts; and I will give to each one of you according to your deeds. But I say to you, the rest who are in Thyatira, who do not hold this teaching, who have not known the deep things of Satan, as they call them — I place no other burden on you. Nevertheless what you have, hold fast until I come. And he who overcomes, and he who keeps My deeds until the end, to him I will give authority over the nations; and he shall rule them with a rod of iron, as the vessels of the potter are broken to pieces, as I also have received authority from My Father; and I will give him the morning star. He who has an ear, let him hear what the Spirit says to the churches.

Lovingly,
The Son of God

Revelation 2:18-29

THE CITY

> The working world we live in has its own "trade guilds": pressures to conform, to be dishonest, etc.

It is interesting that the longest letter written in this series of the letters to the seven churches in Revelation 2 and 3 is written to the smallest and least important of all of the seven cities. Thirty-five to forty miles southeast of Pergamum lies the city of Thyatira. It is located at the mouth of a long valley which connects the valleys of the Hermus and Caicus rivers. Through it ran a trade route that started in Pergamum and went all the way to Syria.

However, she was not well known for trade, but for manufacturing, and especially industries having to do with cloth — weaving, dyeing, making garments, etc. When the Apostle Paul was in Philippi, he met Lydia, a woman from Thyatira who sold purple cloth (Acts 16:14).

Some Differences. Some of the things that were significant in the backgrounds of Ephesus, Smyrna and Pergamum are not found in Thyatira. For instance, she is not a city of any special religious importance. There are some pagan gods, namely Artemis and Apollo, whose idols were there. The guardian god of the city was Tyrimnos, who was identified with Apollo. Caesar was considered Apollo incarnate, and worship of him was merged with that of Apollo and both were called sons of Zeus. Christians did not face any particular pressure connected with the worship of these gods.

Thyatira was not a special center for Caesar worship, which meant Christians did not face persecution for refusing to participate in emperor worship. Thyatira's one religious claim to fame was the shrine of an oriental sibyl called the Sambathe, and many people came to that shrine to consult the oracle. The Christians in Thyatira did not suffer because of the pagan religions or emperor worship as we have seen in other cities. The Christians were not free of dangers; however, Thyatira had its own set of hazards.

The Trade Guilds. Thyatira was an important manufacturing city and the center of the trade guilds. Trade guilds were organizations formed around people who practiced certain occupations. Wool workers, linen workers, makers of winter garments, dyers, leather workers, tanners, potters, etc., would each have their own guild.

The trade guilds were religious in nature. Each guild had its own god, a guardian god who was supposed to bless those who were members of that guild. To be able to make a living at any trade in Thyatira, one had to belong to that trade's guild, and in order to belong to that guild, he had to participate in the feasts of the guild gods.

There were three parts to the feasts of the guild gods. First, a cup of wine was poured out to symbolize honor and worship to the god. Then a meal was eaten, part of which had been offered in sacrifice to that god. After the meal when most in attendance were drunk there was an orgy, a sexual free-for-all in which all were expected to participate. In order to be a member of that trade guild, a person had to participate in these feasts, and none of the activities could be avoided without incurring persecution. Obviously, the Christian was put in a terrible situation — participate in these ungodly celebrations, or lose his livelihood. With this background we can better understand what the Lord writes to the church at Thyatira.

SALUTATION AND SELF-DESIGNATION, 2:18

Son of God. The self-designation in the letter to Thyatira is unique. "These are the words of the Son of God." This is the only letter where direct identification is made. In the first three letters the identification has been indirect with descriptions from the original vision recorded in chapter 1. Perhaps this address is to contrast the true Son of God with Thyatira's false gods, the sons of Zeus.

Description. Like the other letters, however, description is added from the vision recorded in chapter 1, "whose eyes are like blazing fire and whose feet are like burnished bronze." "Eyes like blazing fire" would signify burning penetration — the penetrating

> The Lord who has eyes like a flame of fire looks into the inside and sees things that do not appear on the outside.

power of the Lord to see through deception to the inner person. We will see the significance of that later. The feet like burnished bronze may have to do with bronze which has been refined by fire, and some believe it alludes to one of the major trade guilds. Another view is that it gives the idea of strength and splendor.

> He that overcomes is he who keeps the Lord's works until the end.

COMMENDATION, 2:19

Their Works. The Lord begins, as is customary, with words of commendation: "I know your deeds, your love and faith, your service and perseverance, and that you are now doing more than you did at first." The commendation to Thyatira is similar to that directed to Ephesus, i.e., there is a construction in the Greek that we do not see in the English. The words connected by the epexegetic "and" describe what the "works" were, rather than being additional items. We could read verse 19 this way: "I know your works, that is your work of love, your work of faith, your work of ministry, and your work of patience."

Greater than the First. Notice the contrast between what was said to the Ephesians and what is said here. The Ephesians had left their first love and were told to go back to doing the first works; Thyatira is told that their present works are even greater than their first works. The Lord's words are quite a tribute to that church. If we knew nothing else about the church at Thyatira, we would think nothing could be wrong with a church which was described in that way.

But the Lord who has eyes like a flame of fire looks into the inside and sees things that do not appear on the outside. Perhaps an important lesson for us to glean from these letters is that a church might have many things good about it, yet still have characteristics which need correction.

CONDEMNATION, 2:20-21

Nevertheless, I have this against you: You tolerate that

woman Jezebel, who calls herself a prophetess. By her teaching she misleads my servants into sexual immorality and the eating of food sacrificed to idols. I have given her time to repent of her immorality, but she is unwilling.

Jezebel. Some may say there is nothing in a name, but do you know anyone who has named her daughter "Jezebel"? The name has such a negative connotation that even people with little or no knowledge of the Bible know what it means. It has taken a place in our dictionaries as a word which means a shameless and evil woman.

The story of Jezebel is found in 1 Kings chapters 16 through 21, and 2 Kings 9. Ahab, king of Israel, married Jezebel, daughter of the king of Sidon. Her father, Ethbaal, had been high priest of Baal until he murdered the king and took the throne. Perhaps that background contributed to her bloodthirsty, power-hungry nature and to her zeal for Baal. She introduced Baal worship into Israel and caused the Israelites to fall away from God.

Her influence corrupted Judah as well, when her daughter Athaliah married Jehoram, king of Judah. The whole of the divided kingdom was under her evil influence for a long period of its history as first she and Ahab and then two of her sons ruled Israel, and her grandson Ahaziah and his mother ruled Judah.

Jezebel's intention was to eliminate the worship of Jehovah, and she waged a fierce campaign against his prophets. Elijah dealt a severe blow to Baal worship in the confrontation on Mt. Carmel, which resulted in the deaths of 450 prophets of Baal (1 Kings 18:16-40). However, Jezebel was far from beaten and threatened Elijah's life, causing him to flee.

> What the Lord had against the church at Thyatira was their toleration of those who put forth the false teaching.

Her power and ruthlessness were also demonstrated in her ability to involve the elders and nobles of Samaria in a conspiracy to take the life and property of Naboth when Ahab pouted about wanting the property for a garden (1 Kings 21:1ff). That event resulted in Elijah's prophecy that Jezebel would die in a grisly and dishonorable manner, and the account of that death is recorded in 2 Kings 9:30-37.

The Jezebel at Thyatira. Who was the Jezebel at Thyatira? There are several viewpoints. Some have suggested she was the sibyl Sambathe, but it is not likely that a sibylline priestess could have wielded that much influence in the church. Another idea is that she was Lydia, the seller of purple whom Paul met and converted in Philippi, but there is no reason for making such a connection. A third view based on a variant reading is that she was the wife of the preacher or one of the leaders of the church at Thyatira. It is not likely that the variant reading is correct, so that identification is doubtful. Others would say she was just a prominent woman in the church who had a lot of negative influence.

> **There will always be an effort by some to mix Christianity with worldly activities hoping for the benefits of both.**

This author's view is that the Jezebel of Thyatira was not a person, but the personification of a teaching or doctrine that encouraged people to compromise their Christian beliefs and participate in the activities of the trade guild feasts.

What the Lord had against the church at Thyatira was their toleration of those who put forth that doctrine. They were allowing a teaching which resulted not only in acts of sin, but also in an alliance with paganism. It may have been an attractive idea to the Christians at Thyatira because participating in the trade guild feasts would protect their occupations, and that made the teaching all the more insidious. There was no repentant attitude in spite of the Lord's patience, and perhaps for that reason the threatened judgment was severe.

Jezebelism is still with us today, and so is the toleration. *There will always be an effort by some to mix Christianity with worldly activities hoping for the benefits of both.* And there will always be some who are tolerant of such, not wanting their peace disturbed with negative preaching or confrontation with error. The Lord's judgment on Thyatira should give us some idea how he might feel about that kind of influence in the church today.

WARNING AND JUDGMENT, 2:22-23

So I will cast her on a bed of suffering, and I will make those who commit adultery with her suffer intensely, unless they repent of her ways. I will strike her children dead. Then all the churches will know that I am he who searches hearts and minds, and I will repay each of you according to your deeds.

The Jezebelites may have been enjoying the bed of fornication — compromise with immoral pagan practices, but the Lord says their punishment will be the bed of affliction. Disease as punishment for sin was an accepted view, as seen in the results of the Corinthians' misuse of the Lord's Supper (1 Cor. 11:27-29).

Those who cooperated in that doctrine would suffer great tribulation — intense suffering — if they did not repent. "Her children," perhaps those who were led astray, would be "killed with death," a Hebraism that probably means "killed by pestilence." It is possible that the reference to "children" alludes to the slaying of the sons of Ahab as Israel was purged of that family's evil influence.

The persuasive logic of the Jezebelites may have confused many in the church, but he who has eyes like a flame of fire saw through to the hearts and minds, identified the guilty and was going to repay each man for what he had done. *A church that in some ways was working* — loving, faithful, ministering, and patient — *had the serious problem of tolerating evil*, and that evil was going to be corrected.

EXHORTATION AND PROMISE, 2:24-29

Now I say to the rest of you in Thyatira, to you who do not hold to her teaching, and have not learned Satan's so-called deep secrets (I will not impose any other burden on you): Only hold on to what you have until I come [vv. 24, 25].

Hold on to what you have. The Lord addresses the faithful, those who have not been a part of the heresy, with words of encouragement. Some had

> A church that in some ways was working had the serious problem of tolerating evil.

not accepted this doctrine — had not known "Satan's so-called deep secrets." That expression probably refers to the Jezebelism, and "so-called" likely means the faithful referred to the teaching as the deep things of Satan. The Lord knows they have heavy burdens to bear and he is not going to increase that burden. In fact, he exhorts them to continue to be faithful in the face of the difficulties — "tie a knot in the end of the rope and hold on." The promise of his coming reminds them that they will be rewarded.

> **Jesus told his followers that they would live with him in a special place that had been prepared for them.**

To the Overcomer. The overcoming passage to Thyatira reads,

> To him who overcomes and does my will to the end, I will give authority over the nations — He will rule them with an iron scepter; he will dash them to pieces like pottery — just as I have received authority from my Father. I will also give him the morning star [vv. 26-28].

We learn something about overcoming here that was not specifically stated in the earlier letters. The Lord says *he that overcomes is he who keeps the Lord's works until the end.* That is a good definition of what it means to overcome. It was expressed another way in the letter to the church in Smyrna when they were told to be "faithful unto death," Rev. 2:10.

Verses 26b and 27 are a rendering of Psalm 2:8-9, which has always been understood to be messianic. Rev. 12:5 and 19:15 use the same imagery, applied to the victorious Christ. The verb means "to shepherd" and the sense of the verse is the Lord will shepherd with an iron staff which can destroy sinners like a clay pot can be broken into pieces. Christ will give the overcomer a share of that authority which the Father had given him (Matt. 28:18), and Christ and his followers will have absolute power over the sinful nations.

Christians today can wield power over the nations as they pray for the leaders (1 Tim. 2:1-3) and intercede with the God of Heaven as he rules this world.

The overcomer is made another promise: "and I will give him the morning star." There are many views as to the identification of the "morning star." One is that it alludes to Lucifer of Isa. 14:12. Another ties it in with the immortality of the righteous in Dan. 12:3. It has been defined as the dawn of eternal life — that resurrection from darkness into light as the morning star rises over the darkness of the night.

It is most likely to be the promise of the Christ, who identifies himself as the bright, morning star in Rev. 22:16. The overcomer is given the greatest promise of all — the Lord himself. John 14:1ff records *Jesus telling his followers that they would live with him in a special place that had been prepared for them.* Those words would have been of immeasurable comfort and strength to the Christians at Thyatira and would have helped them be steadfast in the face of severe pressures. If they continued to rise above those pressures, they would be victorious and live and rule with Christ himself.

The message is one of strength and comfort to Christians today as well. *The working world we live in has its own "trade guilds": pressures to conform, pressures to be dishonest, pressures to be immoral, pressures to make wrong judgments, etc.* We must hold fast as the Christians in Thyatira were exhorted to do, and the rewards they were promised will be ours.

REFLECTING ON THYATIRA

1. What "Jezebels" have you encountered or heard about today? What is our responsibility in reference to them?

2. How was Thyatira different from the cities already mentioned? How the same?

3. What similar situations might we face today to the requirements of the Thyatiran trade guilds?

4. Why are the eyes of John's vision of Jesus mentioned with significance here?

5. Compare the progression at Thyatira to the progression at Ephesus. In which direction is your congregation going?

6. How can a Christian wield authority even today, before Christ returns?

7. What are some things we need to hold fast to that we might be in danger of losing?

8. Make a summary of this letter, as you did of the others. Remember to use your own words as much as possible.

5
FIVE

SARDIS
BE GOOD ON THE INSIDE

The Church
Sardis
Asia Minor

Dear Brethren,
　I know your deeds, that you have a name that you are alive, but you are dead. Wake up, and strengthen the things that remain, which were about to die; for I have not found your deeds completed in the sight of My God. Remember therefore what you have received and heard; and keep it, and repent. If therefore you will not wake up, I will come like a thief, and you will not know at what hour I will come upon you. But you have a few people in Sardis who have not soiled their garments; and they will walk with Me in white; for they are worthy. He who overcomes shall thus be clothed in white garments; and I will not erase his name from the book of life, and I will confess his name before My Father, and before His angels. He who has an ear, let him hear what the Spirit says to the churches.

　　　　　　　　　　Lovingly,
　　　　　　　　　　He who has the seven Spirits of God,
　　　　　　　　　　and the seven stars

Revelation 3:1-6

THE CITY

Sardis had been the capital of the ancient kingdom of Lydia, but was declining by the time of the Romans. She was located thirty miles southeast of Thyatira and about fifty miles northeast of Ephesus. She is historically significant as being the city from where Xerxes invaded Greece, and where Cyrus marched against Croesus.

> **Sardis was a church at peace, but the peace she enjoyed was the peace of the dead.**

The city overlooked the valley of the Hermus, and the trade of the valley centered there. Five roads converged at Sardis which gave her commercial advantage, and she was the center of a thriving woolen industry.

The major religion of the city was worship of the goddess Cybele, and the rituals involved in that worship were frenzied, hysterical affairs. Fortunately, Christians did not face serious pressure to participate in these pagan activities. Emperor worship was not consequential enough to pose a threat to Christians.

If Sardis had a claim to fame, it was decadence. Even in the pagan world, Sardis was thought of with contempt. Because of the trade and industry there was a lot of wealth in the city, and that wealth brought about an emphasis on pleasure and luxury. Sardis was described by the people of her day as a loose-living, pleasure-loving, luxury-laden city.

The Christians at Sardis suffered none of the persecutions faced by the other churches. There was no threat from Caesar worship or pressure to engage in pagan ceremonies. There was no danger from the slander of influential Jews. There was no economic peril from trade guilds. There was not even the hint of any internal heresy within the church. The church at Sardis was completely free from trouble both without and within. *She was a church at peace, but the peace she enjoyed was the peace of the dead.*

SALUTATION AND SELF-DESIGNATION, 3:1

"These are the words of him who holds the seven spirits of

God, and the seven stars." That description from the vision recorded in chapter one identifies the writer as the Lord Jesus Christ. "The seven spirits" probably signifies the full range of divine power (see the NIV footnote, "sevenfold Spirit"), and "the seven stars" the seven churches. The Lord is full of power and wisdom and might, and he holds in his hand the destiny of the church at Sardis, even as he does all the churches.

COMMENDATION, 3:1a

"I know your deeds; you have a reputation of being alive . . ." There is little to commend this church. They are a church that has a name — they had a good reputation — but they did not live up to that name. Outwardly they gave the appearance of being a faithful, active congregation, but it was in name only.

There are several factors which may have contributed to a good reputation. The church at Sardis may have had a large membership. Perhaps the church at Sardis was one of the big churches in the brotherhood in Asia Minor. There is a certain distinction attached to large numbers — an attitude that equates a large membership with a fine church. If so many people attend there, it must have much to commend it.

She may have had a name because of wealth. Considering the commerce and industry in Sardis and the reputation the city itself had for riches and luxury, the church there could have been affluent. In societies that respect wealth and position a congregation of wealthy high-placed people might well have a high standing in the community.

> It is not what we think about ourselves or what others may think of us, but what the Lord thinks that is important.

It is possible that an attractive worship service contributed to the good name of the church at Sardis. Perhaps people enjoyed attending there because the beauty and structure of the service appealed to them.

Sardis may have had a good reputation because she had sound teachers. We do not read of Balaamites there, or Nicolaitans, or a Jezebel. There were none of those that called themselves to be apostles but were found not to be so.

> **A church is in danger of death when it begins to worship its past.**

These things might contribute to the outward appearance of a church and give it a good reputation. Sardis had such a name, but the Lord said that name was unfounded. *We see again that it is not what we think about ourselves, or even what others may think about us, but what the Lord thinks about us that is important.*

CONDEMNATION, 3:1b

"You are dead." The church at Sardis was alive in name only — she was dead in works. Sardis was living in the past — basking in a reputation they may have deserved at one time, but no longer. They may have been alive and vibrant in a material sense, but they were dead or dying spiritually. We will see that there remained a few faithful Christians at Sardis, but apparently the majority had so compromised with the environment of the decadent city they were Christians in name only.

What could cause a church to be in danger of death? What are the danger signs — the signals we need to look for in a church to see if it is terminally ill?

Living in the Past. A church is in danger of death when it begins to worship its past; when it lives on memories instead of taking stock of the present and planning for the future. It is easy to sit back comfortably, to focus on traditions and past accomplishments, to be self-satisfied with the way things have always been done and resist change and new ideas. A church that lives on what it has done, instead of what it is doing and will do, is dead.

Sardis was not a defunct church with a dilapidated building about to close its doors. Its membership was not dwindling and the preacher ready to resign. They could not have had a good reputation unless they had given every appearance of being a thriving congregation. They probably met regularly and had committees galore with lots of activities going on which made it appear to be an active church. But it had no such reputation with the Lord.

All Form and no Spirit. A church is in danger of dying when it is more concerned with the forms — the ritual — than it is with the spirit. We can concentrate on the order of worship to the exclusion of worship itself. Church members can get so accustomed to a traditional pattern in the service they object to any variation, putting their faith in the form rather than in the spirit of worship. *When brethren are more concerned about the form than they are about the true meaning of worship, the church is in danger of dying.*

Materialism. A church's health is threatened when it is more concerned with the material than it is with the spiritual — more concerned about the cost than the lost. People can be more disturbed over what may be going on in the fellowship hall than they are that there are people dying in a lost condition. Elaborate building projects and expensive programs can get in the way of preaching the Gospel or feeding the hungry. When a church is more concerned about material things than spiritual things, it has lost a God-designed perspective. The church at Sardis may have been infected with the materialistic attitude of the city around it, and that is a real danger in our time as well.

EXHORTATION AND WARNING, 3:2-3

Be watchful. "Wake up! Strengthen what remains and is about to die, for I have not found your deeds complete in the sight of my God." Being watchful would have important significance to the people of Sardis. The city was situated on the side of a hill and surrounded on three sides by steep cliffs. She was well-defended against her enemies if the people kept watch. Herodotus, an early Greek historian, tells us of a time when lack of watchfulness caused the city's downfall. In 549 B.C. Cyrus came through the area

> When brethren are more concerned about the form than the true meaning of worship, the church is in danger of dying.

on a campaign and intended to take Sardis quickly and move on. He promised a reward to the soldier who could devise a way to get into the city. One of Cyrus' soldiers happened to see a guard up on the cliff drop his helmet, scale down the wall to retrieve it, and scale back up. That night Cyrus' men used that same method and entered the city successfully because there was no guard on duty. The people of Sardis had become complacent because they believed their position to be impregnable, so they were not watchful.

> The warning to be watchful applies to Christians today as it did to those in Sardis.

In 216 B.C., it happened again. Antiochus the Great took the city when a Cretan named Lagoras found a vulnerable spot and led a band of men on a daring climb into the city. The city had been taken twice because of a lack of vigilance. With that in their history, being told to "be watchful" would catch their attention. *The warning to be watchful applies to Christians today it did to those in Sardis.* There are two areas in which it is important to be watchful. The first area is one's weak points. Each Christian knows where he is the weakest, the most vulnerable to temptation, and he needs to stand guard.

A Christian needs also to be watchful in his strong points. Paul said, "So, if you think you are standing firm, be careful that you don't fall" (1 Cor. 10:12). Sometimes a Christian will not put up any guard at all in those areas where he feels he is strong. Satan attacks on all fronts, so the Christian must be watchful on all fronts.

Strengthen the Things that Remain. The church at Sardis was told to "strengthen what remains and is about to die, for I have not found your deeds complete in the sight of my God." *Sardis may have been declared dead, but there was hope of restoration to life.* There were some good characteristics and some good works which were ready to die, but they still had a spark of life. None of these good works had been completed, or carried out fully. In other words, breathe life into these dry bones. If we visited the church at Sardis they would give us a tour of the building to show us how good things were.

Their membership would be large, their finances in good shape, and we would see a lot of activity. But theirs is quantity without quality. The salt had lost its saltiness. They had a reputation that they were alive, but in reality they were dead.

Sardis is warned to be watchful — to be aware of its failures and to do something about them. She was to strengthen the areas that still had a spark of life and build on them, complete them so the life of the church could be saved.

Remember, Receive and Repent. "Remember, therefore, what you have received and heard; obey it, and repent." In the original language the word "remember" is in the present imperative tense, which expresses continuous action. It carries the idea of "go on remembering" or "remember continually" or "do not forget." The Christians at Sardis no longer kept in mind the spiritual nature of the Gospel to which they had been converted. They had been secularized by the materialism around them and needed to be reminded to go back to emphasizing things of spiritual importance.

They were to remember what they had received. The word "received" is in the perfect tense, and means something that was received and is still in their possession. They had heard the Gospel of Christ, had received it in faith and obedience, and had obtained the salvation that comes through that Gospel. It was still in their possession, and remembering it should call them back to their original priorities.

"Repent" is in the aorist imperative tense which implies a definite action completed in the past. It may point to the specific time when they first heard the Gospel and turned from sin to Christ. They are to take that specific action now and turn from their dead spiritual condition back to Jesus with their former enthusiasm and zeal for spiritual things.

The Christians in Ephesus were also told to remember and repent (2:5). The point was made there that *the road back begins with remembering.* Newly converted Christians are excited and zealous about the things they can do for the Lord. Their lives have a new spiritual emphasis as they revel in the relation-

Sardis may have been declared dead, but there was hope of restoration to life.

ship they now have with the Lord. The church at Sardis was told to remember those things and turn back to them.

> **The road back begins with remembering.**

Or I Will Come. "But if you do not wake up, I will come like a thief, and you will not know at what time I will come to you." The phrase "come like a thief" is used in other places in the New Testament to describe the coming of the Lord as unexpected — with no warning (1 Thess. 5:2; 2 Pet. 3:10). The Second Coming is not being discussed here because that is not contingent upon the actions of the church at Sardis. What is being discussed is judgment that will come upon that church if it does not repent. They will suffer the consequences for their failures and spiritual death, and when it does come, it will be swift and unexpected.

PROMISE, 3:4-6

> Yet you have a few people in Sardis who have not soiled their clothes. They will walk with me, dressed in white, for they are worthy. He who overcomes will, like them, be dressed in white. I will never blot out his name from the book of life, but will acknowledge his name before my Father and his angels.

There were still a few in Sardis who had not been contaminated — who had kept themselves pure from pagan and worldly influences. We see that it is possible for a minority to remain faithful and be acceptable to God even when the majority is not. These Christians were "the salt of the earth" and as such kept the spark of life alive in the church at Sardis. To these faithful the Lord gives four precious promises.

Walk With Me. There is no more glorious promise than that the faithful Christian will dwell in the presence of his Lord. In John 14:1ff the Lord said he was going to prepare a place for his disciples, and where he was, they would be also. Paul knew that to leave this body meant to be at home with the Lord (2 Cor. 4:8). He encouraged the Thessalonians by telling them they would be with the Lord forever (1 Thess. 4:17). In Revelation 7 the Great Multitude is pictured as being before the throne of God, and in the presence of the Lamb who is their Shepherd and shall guide them to fountains of waters of life, verse 17.

The Lord told the faithful in Sardis they would walk with him — they would know the joy of being in his presence. Surely they were strengthened by this promise and better equipped to overcome.

Dressd in White. Those who had not defiled their garments — the overcomers — would be dressed in white. Seven times in the book of Revelation saints are seen in white garments: 3:6, 18; 4:4; 6:11; 7:9, 13 and 19:14. White symbolized purity, and was also significant as the garment worn by a victorious contestant. Purity is likely the primary thought here with perhaps a secondary application to the victory of those who overcome. Those who kept themselves pure from the defilements of paganism and worldliness would be in the presence of the Lord, dressed in the white garments that represented their purity. They were worthy because they had kept themselves pure and done nothing to forfeit their salvation.

Book of Life. Our first introduction to a divine register is in Exod. 32:32-33 when Moses asks the Lord to forgive the Israelites, or if not, to blot him out of "the book you have written." Jehovah replies he will only blot those who have sinned out of his book. In Ps. 69:28 David asks that his enemies be blotted out of the book of life. Daniel was told that in a time of great distress everyone whose name was found written in the book would be delivered, Dan. 12:1. "The book" was a register of God's people, a roll of the faithful.

In ancient history it was customary to record a person's birth in the city records and then blot that name out when he died. If a criminal's name was removed from the civic register, he lost his citizenship.

> Those in Sardis who had compromised and who were dead, were in danger of having their names blotted out of the book of life.

Those in Sardis who had compromised and who were dead, were in danger of having their names blotted out of the book of life — being removed from the roll of God's people — losing their citizenship in the kingdom. But the faithful were in no such danger. Their names would not be blotted out; they would retain the status of citizen..

> Individuals need to ask themselves if they are among the faithful few.

Names Confessed Before the Father and His Angels. The overcomer's name will be confessed before the Father and his angels. In Matt. 10:32 the Lord said if anyone confessed him before men, he would confess that one before his Father. What an inestimable blessing it will be. Jesus will say, "Father, this one is mine; this one is faithful and should be admitted into our presence." We can hardly comprehend the significance of that. Think of the blessing of being that overcomer who walks with the Lord in white, whose name is written in the book of Life, and whose name the Lord Jesus in Heaven confesses to the Father.

Sardis was a church in a lot of trouble but not without hope. And even in the midst of a majority that was spiritually dead, there was a faithful minority. That faithful minority was encouraged by the wonderful promises to the overcomer. Being faithful under pressure now meant to be rewarded beyond measure in the life to come.

The lessons in this letter can be applied in two ways. First, congregations of the Lord's people need to take stock and make sure they are not living on a past reputation instead of staying spiritually alive. It is important to be more concerned about what the Lord thinks about us than what other people think about us.

Secondly, *individuals need to ask themselves if they are among the faithful few.* Have we made a covenant with God to be faithful even if others are not — to be pure even if others are not — to do what is right no matter what others do? Sometimes it takes a lot of courage to make decisions like that because the Christian faces daily pressures to conform to the world's standards. We need to remember the promises made to the overcomers in Sardis and to be confident the rewards will far outweigh any difficulties we might face as a result of taking a stand for the Lord.

REFLECTING ON SARDIS

1. What were the influences of Sardis on the church there? What are some present-day parallels?

2. Can you think of churches today that have undeserved reputations?

3. Are we in danger of living in the past? What is the difference between learning from the past and living in it?

4. What lesson from the past could the city of Sardis use about watchfulness? What is the spiritual significance of this historical and political lesson?

5. Is there a connection between large churches and materialism? Does there have to be?

6. How can we best keep our garments white? What does this mean, exactly?

7. Some claim that it is impossible for a Christian, once saved, to be lost. Does the implied warning against having our names blotted from the book of life say anything about this issue?

8. How would you summarize the warnings and promises of this fifth letter?

SIX

PHILADELPHIA
TAKE THE OPEN DOOR

The Church
Philadelphia
Asia Minor

Dear Brethren,

I know your deeds, Behold, I have put before you an open door which no one can shut, because you have a little power, and have kept My word, and have not denied My name. Behold, I will cause those of the synagogue of Satan, who say that they are Jews, and are not, but lie — behold, I will make them to come and bow down at your feet, and to know that I have loved you. Because you have kept the word of My perseverance, I also will keep you from the hour of testing, that hour which is about to come upon the whole world, to test those who dwell upon the earth. I am coming quickly; hold fast what you have, in order that no one take your crown. He who overcomes, I will make him a pillar in the temple of My God, and he will not go out from it anymore; and I will write upon him the name of My God, and the name of the city of My God, the new Jerusalem, which comes down out of heaven from My God, and My new name. He who has an ear, let him hear what the Spirit says to the churches.

Lovingly,
He who is holy, who is true,
who has the key of David

Revelation 3:7-13

THE CITY

Location. Philadelphia, the city of brotherly love, was located twenty-eight miles southeast of Sardis, eighty miles due east of Smyrna. Strategically located, Philadelphia was at the border of three different countries, Mysia, Lydia and Phrygia. She served as a central point through which Greek culture would be funnelled toward the east in the ancient world. Because of her particular position geographically, she became known as the "Gateway to the East."

History. Herodotus relates a tradition about the place where Philadelphia one day would stand. When the Persian king Xerxes was on his way to invade Europe, he found shelter at this spot under a tree. He admired and appreciated the tree so much he decked it with costly gifts and left a personal bodyguard there to look after it. It was on this spot some years later that Philadelphia was built.

Philadelphia is not as old a city as the other ones we have studied, dating back to about 150 years before Christ. Her name was taken from Attalus II, whose loyalty to his brother Eumenes resulted in his being called "Philadelphus," or "brother-lover."

She was founded for the purpose of spreading the Greek language, the Greek culture, and the Greek manner into the east. She was intended to be a missionary city — to promote Hellenism in the land.

Prosperity. Philadelphia lay on the edge of a great volcanic plain, one of the most fertile areas in the world. She was world-famous for her wines and enjoyed an extensive market which brought much prosperity.

The volcanic area also created numerous hot springs which were renowned for their healing powers. People came from far and wide to bathe in the medicinal waters, and this steady flow of visitors added to the wealth of the city.

> "What he opens no one can shut, and what he shuts no one can open."

The very feature which brought good fortune to the people of Philadelphia also brought danger. Because of the volcanic nature of the area, it was subject to frequent earthquakes. The people lived an unsettled life, and at least once, the city had been laid waste.

> **Access to the heavenly palace is through Jesus and none other.**

SALUTATION AND SELF-DESIGNATION, 3:7

"These are the words of him who is holy and true, who holds the key of David. *What he opens no one can shut, and what he shuts no one can open.*" The self-designation addressed to the church in Philadelphia is unique. In the other six letters to the churches of Asia the Lord identifies himself with descriptions we see from chapter one, but that language is not drawn on for the identification to the Philadelphians.

"He that is true," is a very significant phrase. There are two words for "true" in the original language. *Alethes* refers to something that is true as opposed to something that is false. *Alethinos* means something which is genuine as opposed to that which is counterfeit. The second is the word used here. The Lord is saying he is real — genuine — not an illusion or counterfeit.

"He who holds the key of David." The Lord draws on a passage from the prophet Isaiah to further identify himself. From Isaiah 22 we learn that Eliakim, the faithful steward of Hezekiah, was given the key to the royal palace. He completely controlled access to the palace and to the presence of the king. Anyone who would enter had to go through him. In speaking of Eliakim, Isaiah writes in verse 22, "I will place on his shoulder the key to the house of David; what he opens no one can shut, and what he shuts no one can open." Jesus here describes himself as one who has the authority to open and close the door. *Access to the heavenly palace and its king is through Jesus and none other.* In John 14:6 Jesus said, "I am the way and the truth and the life. No one comes to the Father except through me."

COMMENDATION, 3:8

"I know your deeds. See, I have placed before you an open

door that no one can shut. I know that you have little strength, yet you have kept my word and have not denied my name."

Little Strength. It is possible the church at Philadelphia was referred to as having "little strength" because it was a small congregation and did not have much impact on the city. In spite of their little strength they had been faithful, and that had not gone unnoticed by their Lord. Every one of the letters to the seven churches has an "I know" statement. It is important for us to remember that the Lord knows what is happening, both with the church collectively and with Christians individually.

The Open Door. The parenthetical phrase "see, I have placed before you an open door . . ." has been interpreted various ways. The most common explanation is in a missionary context. Paul uses this particular language, for instance, in 1 Cor. 16:9 when he says, "because a great door for effective work has opened to me." In 2 Cor. 2:12 he says that in Troas, "the Lord had opened a door for me." He asks the Colossians to pray for him and his companions that "God may open a door for our message" (Col. 4:3).

Perhaps the term is even more meaningful in light of Philadelphia's geographical location. As the "Gateway to the East," situated at the eastern end of a valley leading to the great central plain, it had a unique opportunity to carry the Gospel to the cities beyond. It would have been significant and encouraging to this church, perhaps small and not very strong, that the Lord was going to present them with greater opportunities for service.

Christians today need to be watchful for doors of opportunity. It behooves us to (1) ask the Lord to open doors of opportunity for service, and (2) be ready to go through those doors when they are opened. Sometimes doors of opportunity are opened unexpectedly, and a walk of faith is necessary to get us through the door.

> Christians today need to be watchful for doors of opportunity.

Another interpretation also fits the context. The preceding verse referred to the door of the kingdom which Christ alone could open and shut. The following verses speak of the Jews of the "synagogue of Satan" and suggest that the Christians had suffered at their hands. It is possible that Jews who were converted to Christianity were then excommunicated — the doors of the synagogue shut to them. Jesus could be telling them it does not matter that the doors of the synagogue are closed to them — he has opened the door of the kingdom for them, and no man can shut that door.

> The Christians may have been in a difficult situation, but Christ himself is their access to their reward.

It is possible that the door refers to Jesus himself. In the parable of the Good Shepherd in John 10, Jesus said he was the door to the sheepfold (verses 7 and 9). In the ancient world, sheep were often gathered into an enclosed area at the close of the day. Sometimes there was no door — simply an opening in the enclosure. The shepherd would lie down in the opening and be the door himself so that nothing could get in or out except through him. *The Christians in Philadelphia may have been in a difficult situation, but they are reassured that Christ himself is their access to their reward.*

Kept His Word. The church at Philadelphia had faithfully kept the Lord's word and not denied his name in spite of their little power and whatever difficulties they faced. Pergamum received similar praise (2:13). Being obedient to the word of the Lord is how we show our love for him (John 14:15). We will be judged according to that word (John 12:48-50). It is that word that is "useful for teaching, rebuking, correcting and training in righteousness, so that the man of God may be thoroughly equipped for every good work" (2 Tim. 3:16-17). Faithfulness to that word is understood in Rev. 2:10. "Be faithful, even to the point of death, and I will give you the crown of life."

In spite of pressures brought to bear upon them, in spite of their "little power," the Christians in Philadelphia had remained faithful. Their faithfulness would be rewarded.

FUTURE REWARDS, 3:9-12

Victory Over Foes. One of the future rewards of the faithful is going to be victory over their foes. In verse 9 Jesus says, "I will make those who are of the synagogue of Satan, who claim to be Jews though they are not, but are liars — I will make them come and fall down at your feet and acknowledge that I have loved you."

The church in Philadelphia was apparently having some of the same kind of difficulties that faced the Christians in Smyrna. The Jews of the day thought they were the people of God, and mistreated Christians in the name of religion. The time will come when those Jews will acknowledge the Christ and his love for his church, and the faithful Christians will be vindicated.

The Hour of Trial. "Since you have kept my command to endure patiently, I will also keep you from the hour of trial that is going to come upon the whole world to test those who live on the earth." The Christians in Philadelphia had kept the Lord's command to endure patiently, and as a reward for this they would be kept from the hour of trial that was to come. The Christians in Smyrna were told, "Do not be afraid of what you are about to suffer. I tell you the devil will put some of you in prison to test you, and you will suffer persecuttion for ten days. Be faithful, even to the point of death, and I will give you the crown of life" (2:10).

The Lord is telling the churches in Asia Minor, specifically Smyrna and Philadelphia, that a time of trial is coming — a period of persecution. *God never promised his people that when they become Christians they will be vaccinated against tribulation.* They are not exempt from hard times. When the Lord promises Christians he will keep them during trial, he means that he will see them through it — help them stay faithful through it — and bring about their ultimate victory. Exempting them from tribulation does not fit with the rest of the picture in Revelation.

Later in the book, in chapters 7 and 14, we find the redeemed of God pictured as 144,000 servants who have the seal of God upon their foreheads. They are sealed because they came through persecution and will be vindicated when God brings judgment on the earth. They had to endure the persecution but

> If we remain faithful, we will be vindicated and victorious in the eyes of unbelievers.

because they were faithful through it, they were sealed. In the Judgment they will be signified as belonging to the Lord.

The Lord is telling the Christians in Philadelphia they will be kept because they kept his word. He is the keeper — the holder of the key — and will be the one who keeps them.

In the trial which is about to come upon the Roman Empire, Christians are going to face hard times. There will be many temptations to turn from the faith. But Christ is promising here that faithful followers will be protected and able to persevere during this "hour of trial." The "hour of trial" is not a period of time but a designation of the trial itself. "Those who live on the earth" refers to the non-Christian world (cf. Rev. 11:10).

I am coming soon. "I am coming soon. Hold on to what you have, so that no one will take your crown." The phrase "I am coming soon" indicates the promised judgment is not far off. To further sustain this, John later will write that the things written in this book "must soon take place" (22:6) for "the time is near" (22:10). The crown referred to brings to remembrance the victor's crown which the athletes received if they won at the games. These brethren were already reigning as kings (Rev. 1:5-6), and as victors, were wearing the victory crown which the Lord promised (cf. 2 Tim. 4:8).

A Pillar in the Temple. "Him who overcomes I will make a pillar in the temple of my God." This idea of pillar is very significant. A pillar has one special function; it is to support the edifice of which it forms a part.

The church is the temple of God (1 Cor. 3:16-17), and that ties in with the description of faithful Christians as "pillars." There are at least two ideas involved in pillar. One is incorporation: a pillar is an integral part of the structure to which it belongs. These Christians in Philadelphia are promised they will be an integral part of the heavenly Temple if they overcome. Second is the idea of permanence and stability. They were told they would become part of the temple of God and not go out any more.

This would have special meaning to the people of Philadelphia. As we mentioned in the background material, Philadelphia was built in an area that was volcanic. She was subject to frequent earthquakes which forced the people to flee the city. The people must have lived with some insecurity, never knowing when they would have to leave the city because of an earthquake, or whether the city would be in ruin and uninhabitable when they returned. We can only guess at what this promise meant to them — they were going to be part of the temple of God and would have security, permanence, and stability.

Three Names. Then the Philadelphians are promised a beautiful threefold inscription: (1) "I will write on him the name of my God." That inscription would identify the Christian as belonging to God. (2) "And the name of the city of my God, the new Jerusalem." The Christian not only belongs to God, he is a citizen of the kingdom, the New Jerusalem. (3) "And . . . my new name." The third inscription identifies the Christian as one who has a special relationship with Christ, and perhaps implies that after the Second Coming, when the Christian is freed from the mortal body, he will have fuller knowledge and understanding of the Christ.

What the Spirit Says to the Churches. Churches today must heed what the Spirit says to the churches just as these churches of Asia were told to do. *Being small in number, or having "little power," should not prevent a congregation from taking advantage of the doors that are opened for it.* Even a handful of people can have a mighty impact on society if they are zealous and diligent.

> Being small in number should not prevent a congregation from taking advantage of open doors.

Christians today have the same promises that were made to the church in Philadelphia. *If we remain faithful, we will be vindicated and victorious in the eyes of unbelievers;* we will be "kept" through every trial; we will be a permanent, stable part of the heavenly temple and will be identified as children of God, citizens of the kingdom, and brethren of Christ.

REFLECTING ON PHILADELPHIA

1. What open doors has God placed before you and your congregation?

2. Give the significance of the self-designation of Jesus here.

3. Would you describe your congregation as having only a "little power" or do you know of one that could be so described? How does the unlimited power of God impact on this?

4. What are the possible explanations for the door referred to here?

5. What value does persecution have? Are we actually missing something if we are not persecuted? Explain.

6. How can we reconcile the statement to the first-century church in Philadelphia that Jesus was coming soon with the length of time since then? Research what God says elsewhere about how he views time.

7. What are the modern-day counterparts to the "Jews who were not Jews"?

8. Prepare your personal summary of this letter.

SEVEN

LAODICEA
BE WHOLEHEARTED

The Church
Laodicea
Asia Minor

Dear Brethren,

I know your deeds, that you are neither cold nor hot; I would that you were cold or hot. So because you are lukewarm, and neither hot nor cold, I will spit you out of My mouth. Because you say, "I am rich, and have become wealthy, and have need of nothing," and you do not know that you are wretched and miserable and poor and blind and naked, I advise you to buy from Me gold refined by fire, that you may become rich, and white garments, that you may clothe yourself, and that the shame of your nakedness may not be revealed; and eye salve to anoint your eyes, that you may see. Those whom I love, I reprove and discipline; be zealous therefore, and repent. Behold, I stand at the door and knock; if anyone hears My voice and opens the door, I will come in to him, and will dine with him, and he with Me. He who overcomes, I will grant to him to sit down with Me on My throne, as I also overcame and sat down with My Father on His throne. He who has an ear, let him hear what the Spirit says to the churches.

Lovingly,
The Amen, the faithful and true Witness,
the Beginning of the creation of God

Revelation 3:14-22

There has been a different emphasis in each one of these letters to the seven churches. In the letter to the church at Ephesus, the emphasis was the importance of returning to its first love. The church at Smyrna was warned against compromising and told to be ready to suffer. The emphasis in the letter to Pergamum was the need to champion

> Laodicea had one problem and one problem alone — she was half-hearted in her devotion to God.

the truth in the face of error that was all around them. Thyatira was told to follow righteousness even in the face of evil. The emphasis in the letter to the Christians at Sardis was they should be on the inside what they appear to be on the outside. The letter to the church in Philadelphia stressed the open door of opportunity to evangelize that was available to them in spite of their size. To the church at Laodicea, the emphasis will be a combination of strong denunciation of their complacency and loving appeal for wholeheartedness. This letter is one of the sternest, if not the sternest, of the seven letters.

THE CITY

Forty miles southeast of Philadelphia, three famous cities were clustered in the valley of the Lycus river. To the north of the river was the city of Hierapolis; to the south of the river were the cities of Laodicea and Colosse, about ten miles apart. Laodicea was founded about the middle of the third century B.C. by Antiochus II and named for his wife, Laodice.

Laodicea was the location of a very famous health resort. Hot mineral springs found in the area were reputed to be soothing and restorative. The famous medical center there was the source of a well-known Phrygian eye salve which was in great demand.

Laodicea, having access to a fine soft wool from the black sheep of the valley, was famous for its wool industry. Because of its commercial prosperity, its health resort, and the medical facilities, Laodicea was a popular place for wealthy people to retire. Those things combined to make the city a famous banking center.

The wealth of the city caused her to be proud and self-sufficient, so much so that in A.D. 60 when she suffered a severe earthquake, she refused any outside help in rebuilding the city. We will see that pride, self-sufficiency and dependence upon material wealth were big factors in the Lord's denunciation of the Laodicean church.

The Church at Laodicea. The church at Laodicea is mentioned in Col. 4:16. Paul apparently had written letters to both the church at Colossae and at Laodicea, and in his closing in the letter to the Colossians, he instructs that the two churches exchange and read each other's letters.

The congregation at Laodicea was not infected with the poison of a specific sin, nor was it troubled with either heretics or persecution. *Laodicea had one problem and one problem alone — she was half-hearted in her devotion to God.* There is an important lesson in this letter for the twentieth-century church.

SALUTATION AND SELF-DESIGNATION, 3:14

This letter opens, as do the others, with a phrase that identifies the writer. "These are the words of the Amen, the faithful and true witness, the ruler of God's creation." *Amen.* The word "amen" affirms a statement as being absolutely true, absolutely reliable. We are familiar with statements of Jesus that begin, "verily, verily," or "truly, truly." In the original language it is "*amen, amen*" — coming from Hebrew to Greek to English untranslated. We use "amen" to close prayers, affirming the truth of what has been expressed. Sometimes a preacher's audience will say "amen" to indicate agreement with what has been said.

Jesus refers to himself as "the Amen." In John 14:6 he said he was the way, the truth and the life. *Jesus is not only the one who speaks the truth, he is the truth itself.* The idea is further expanded and defined by the phrase, "the faithful and true witness of God."

The Ruler of God's Creation. "Beginning," as in the older versions, is not the best understanding of the Greek word *arche*. There are some people in the religious world who have taken this passage

> Jesus is the source or origin of all creation.

along with a few others to teach that Jesus was created first, and then he created everything else. That is not what this word means. *Arche* means "source or origin" — *Jesus is the source or origin of all creation.* In Col. 1:15ff, Paul writes that Jesus is preeminent over all creation, all things being created in him through him and unto him. John expressed the same truth in John 1:3, "All things were made through him; and without him nothing was made that has been made." And so, this is Jesus who is true, who is the very source or origin of all things that God has created, who is speaking and writing these words.

CONDEMNATION, 3:15, 17A

The Lord has no words of commendation for the church at Laodicea. Even this first phrase, "I know your deeds," cannot be understood as words of commendation as they were to the church at Ephesus when he told them he knew their deeds and hard work and perseverance, 2:2.

Neither Cold nor Hot. He gets swiftly to the point. "I know your deeds, that you are neither cold [that is, icy cold] nor hot [the word means burning hot]... Because you are lukewarm... I am about to spit you out of my mouth."

This vivid portrayal has long been interpreted against the local background. The city of Hierapolis, six miles across the Lycus valley from Laodicea, was famous for its hot springs. The waters flowed over a wide plateau and were lukewarm by the time they reached the edge. The waters were considered medicinal and beneficial while they were hot but were nauseating when they were lukewarm.

The adjectives "hot" and "cold" are not to be taken as describing spiritual fervor or lack of fervor. The contrast is between the medicinal waters of Hierapolis and the cold pure waters of Colossae, another neighboring city. The hot waters were healing, the cold waters refreshing — both having value to those who drank them.

The church in Laodicea "was providing neither refreshment to the spiritually weary, nor healing for the spiritually sick. It was totally ineffective, and thus distasteful to its Lord" (as cited by Mounce, p. 125). This explanation solves the problem of why the Lord would prefer a church to be "cold" rather than "lukewarm."

Their Claims. The Laodiceans claimed to be rich, to have gotten riches, and to have need of nothing, verse 17. Their were finding their security in their wealth; they were complacent, self-satisfied, and self-sufficient. Not only were they smug in their trust in material wealth, but they also arrogantly claimed to have accomplished it themselves and to need nothing more than what they had been able to gain.

Luke 12:16-21 records a parable of Jesus that speaks to the attitude of the Laodiceans. The Rich Fool taking credit for the bounty and trusting it as his security, was also smug, complacent and self-satisfied as he contemplated his wealth. His wealth did him no good when his soul was required, and that is to be the fate of all who lay up treasure on earth instead of in heaven.

Their True Condition. "But you do not realize that you are wretched, pitiful, poor, blind and naked." Jesus' condemnation directly parallels the reasons for their self-satisfaction. In spite of living in a city noted for its health resort, they were "miserable." They lived in a city noted for its wealth, but they were "poor." Their medical center was world-renowned for its eye salve, but they were "blind." One of their sources of wealth was textiles, yet they were "naked." Their material condition did not keep them from being spiritually destitute, and their reliance upon their material wealth resulted in spiritual poverty.

> **The Lord has no words of commendation for the church at Laodicea.**

The Remedy. "I counsel you to buy from me . . ." The Laodiceans thought they had everything they needed, when in reality, they desperately needed what the Lord had to offer. "Buy from me gold refined in the fire, so you can become rich." They needed the spiritual riches available through Christ to be genuinely rich. "And white clothes to wear, so you can cover your shameful nakedness." In contrast with the black wool of Laodicea's textile industry, the Christians there needed the white robe of righteousness to cover their spiritual nakedness. "And salve to put on your eyes, so you can see." The famous eye salve of Laodicea was not healing their spiritual blindness — they needed the healing of the Lord.

> **It was not the mere possession of wealth which got the Laodiceans into trouble, but the fact that their hope was set on their material riches instead of on God.**

Material wealth is not wrong in and of itself, but it can present a serious danger. Paul addresses this in 1 Timothy 6. Beginning in verse 9 he writes,

> People who want to get rich fall into temptation and a trap and into many foolish and harmful desires that plunge men into ruin and destruction. For the love of money is a root of all kinds of evil. Some people, eager for money, have wandered from the faith and pierced themselves with many griefs.

He continues in verse 17,

> Command those who are rich in this present world not to be arrogant nor to put their hope in wealth, which is so uncertain, but to put their hope in God, who richly provides us with everything for our enjoyment. Command them to do good, to be rich in good deeds, and to be generous and willing to share. In this way they will lay up treasure for themselves as a firm foundation for the coming age, so that they may take hold of the life that is truly life.

It was not the mere possession of wealth which got the Laodiceans into trouble, but the fact that their hope was set on their material riches instead of on God. The remedy was to turn to the Lord for the true riches.

EXHORTATION AND CONCLUSION, 19-22

Tough Love. "Those whom I love, I rebuke and discipline. So be earnest, and repent." "Tough love" is a popular phrase today. It means showing love for another in ways that are best for that person, even if it means correction or reproof or even punishment. The Lord said hard things to the Laodiceans and called for their repentance, but it was out of love for them and a desire for what was best for them.

The word for "love" in this verse is *phileo* — feelings of affection. Jesus is expressing personal affection for them and that love moves him to do what is necessary to bring about a correction of their spiritual deficiencies. Their confidence in his love should motivate them to take his admonitions to heart, just as we can much more easily accept correction from one who loves us than from one who does not have our welfare at heart.

Heb. 12:4-11 compares the chastening of the Lord to the discipline of an earthly father. Out of love for his son a father will discipline him for his good. The loving heavenly Father deals with us as his children as he disciplines us to bring about our righteousness and ultimate well-being. The Hebrew writer goes so far as to say if we are not disciplined by God, we are not children of God.

"Here I am! I stand at the door." Holman Hunt painted a picture of Jesus entitled, "The Light of the World." It pictures Jesus standing and knocking at a door with no knob. The door represents the door of the heart, and the knob is on the inside.

The Lord never forces himself on anybody. He stands and knocks, patiently waiting for the door to be opened and for him to be invited in.

> **The Lord never forces himself on anybody. He stands and knocks, patiently waiting to be invited in.**

"If anyone hears my voice and opens the door, I will come in and eat with him, and he with me." In the ancient world the first two meals of the day were functional — a hurried breakfast at the beginning of the day and some lunch caught during a break from the day's activities. The evening meal, the supper meal, was that time a man spent eating leisurely and socially. The day's activities had been taken care of, and in a relaxed atmosphere he could enjoy dining with his family and friends at a meal that often took hours to eat. In Oriental lands eating together was very significant — it meant a strong bond of affection and companionship. That background caused the common meal to be used as a symbol of the intimacy to be enjoyed in the kingdom of the Lord. The Lord offers that kind of intimacy and fellowship to those who open the door for him.

> "He who has an ear, let him hear what the Spirit says to the churches."

The Promise to the Overcomer. In this last letter as in the other six, there is a promise to the overcomer. "To him who overcomes, I will give the right to sit with me on my throne, just as I overcame and sat down with my Father on his throne." Christ was victorious over Satan and death, and sat down with the Father to reign with him. The Christian is promised the same reward — overcoming persecution and overcoming Satan will result in victory and the opportunity to sit with Christ on his throne and reign with him. Paul writes in 2 Tim. 2:11-12, "Here is a trustworthy saying: If we died with him, we will also live with him; if we endure, we will also reign with him. If we disown him, he will also disown us . . . ."

For the seventh time we read the exhortation, *"He who has an ear, let him hear what the Spirit says to the churches."* The messages to the churches in Asia were not just for them in their time but for the church through the ages. Laodicea had to overcome complacency, materialism, lukewarmness, and dependence on their material wealth. No one can deny that those ills plague the church of today. For the church to overcome and go on to victory, each Christian must overcome the attitudes that diminish enthusiasm and result in stale, lukewarm, or no performance for the Lord. We cannot mistake the call to commitment sent out to each of these seven churches and the same call comes to us. The final reward is worth each Christian's zealous, enthusiastic, faithful service.

REFLECTING ON LAODICEA

1. How did the Laodiceans view themselves? What was their real state?

2. What was the Laodicean church's primary problem? Is this a common problem today? Is it unique to our day or did it happen in the past as well?

3. Would Jesus really prefer a "cold" church to a lukewarm church? If so, what does "cold" mean in that context?

4. What is the remedy for the problem of the Laodicean church? How can we use that remedy today?

5. How does God show His love for us?

6. How intimate a relationship do you have with God? Can you think of ways to improve?

7. Summarize this final letter in your own words.

8. Review the lessons of all seven letters.

About the Author

Edward P. Myers is Professor of Bible and Christian Doctrine, College of Bible and Religion, Harding University in Searcy, Arkansas. He has ministered with Churches of Christ in Texas, Oklahoma, Ohio, West Virginia, and Tennessee.

Myers received his B.A. from Lubbock Christian University, his M.A. from Cincinnati Bible Seminary, his M.T.S. and M.Th. from Southern Christian University, his M.A.R. from Harding University Graduate School of Religion, his D.Min. from Luther Rice Seminary, and his M.Phil. and Ph.D. from Drew University. He is a member of the Evangelical Theological Society, the Society of Biblical Literature, and the Evangelical Philosophical Society.

He has authored *A Study of Angels* and *Evil and Suffering*, both by Howard Publishing, co-authored *Doctrine of the Godhead*, and edited *Biblical Interpretation*, by Baker Book House. Dr. Myers has also published articles in the *Gospel Advocate* and *Restoration Quarterly*.